D1478332

ARCHAEOLOGICAL FIELD METHODS:
AN INTRODUCTION

William S. Dancey
The Ohio State University
Columbus, Ohio

Burgess Publishing Company
Minneapolis, Minnesota

To Mother

Editorial: Jeff Holtmeier, Marta Reynolds, Elisabeth Sövik, Elizabeth S. Weinstein
Production: Morris Lundin, Pat Barnes
Compositor: Gloria Otremba

Cover designed by Adelaide Trettel

Burgess Publishing Company
7108 Ohms Lane
Minneapolis, Minnesota 55435

Preface

This book differs from existing texts on archaeological field method in several ways. In the first place, it deals with methods that have been developed only recently, or that only recently have attracted widespread attention, and which are not covered in detail in other texts. Some examples are probability sampling, aerial photography, systematic surface examination, and flotation techniques. Secondly, although quite a bit of "how to" information is given, the book emphasizes strategy more than tactics. It is concerned more with the design of archaeological field research than with the actual doing of field work. This is most obvious in Chapter 3, which is organized around a general recovery model for prehistory. Thirdly, the book emphasizes archaeological investigation in general rather than any particular type of inquiry. Too commonly, archaeology is thought of as synonymous with excavation. Since there are actually many more ways to acquire archaeological data than by digging, an attempt is made to break away from the excavation stereotype. This will be evident in the discussion of the general recovery model in Chapter 3. It is also for this reason that topics such as the grid system and locational control have been treated in a separate chapter (Chapter 4) rather than in the chapters on archaeological survey and excavation. In all of these ways, the book departs from standard texts and aims for a fresh view of archaeological field method and technique that will also give an accurate description of current practice.

It should be pointed out that the author's personal experience is with the archaeological remains of simple societies in North America in the Holocene Period (the last 10,000 years). The examples in the text, therefore, are drawn largely from this restricted context. The remains of complex societies and of the extremely simple societies of the early Pleistocene Period (2,000,000 to 500,000 years ago) pose special tactical problems that are not addressed directly in this book. Similarly, the investigation of historic sites, wet sites, and submerged sites is not given special treatment.

In general, however, the strategies described should be applicable, with appropriate adjustment, to remains of all types and periods, in all parts of the world. And, though the book reflects an Americanist view of archaeology, other traditions of archaeological research can be accommodated by the approach described here.

Two points should be made regarding the manner of presentation in this text. Divergent points of view are entertained in a number of places. As in any scholarly or scientific field, archaeologists are often at odds with one another about the proper way to do things. Especially in the present decade, when archaeologists are taking a deep, soul-searching look at the goals of the discipline, lack of agreement about methods and techniques is common. Rather than pretend that consensus exists when it does not, different opinions on some subjects have been identified and described. It is only in this way that an accurate picture of the field can be given. In the second place, many of the examples in the text have been summarized in considerable detail. This "mini-case study" approach promotes greater understanding by giving students a feeling for the background and major conclusions of archaeology.

Although responsibility for the final form of this text rests on my shoulders, it could not have been written without the help of others. Many students, directly and indirectly, helped shape the content and commented on various sections. My friend and colleague Frank E. Poirier inspired me to write the book and also read the early drafts. Robert C. Dunnell, Professor and Chairman of the University of Washington Department of Anthropology, will recognize his influence in many parts of the text, particularly in Chapters 2 and 3. Jeff Holtmeier of Burgess Publishing Company provided enthusiastic support and sound advice throughout the project. Mr. Aaron Keirns did a masterly job in preparing the illustrations in Figures. 3.1, 3.2, 3.3, 3.4, 4.2, 4.3, 4.4, 4.7, 4.8, 4.9, 5.3, 5.5, 5.6, 5.7, 5.9, 5.11, and 6.3. Lastly, thanks are due my wife, Jane Dewald, for her encouragement, criticism, and patience.

Contents

Chapter 1

Introduction

A survey of the strategy and tactics of archaeological data recovery presupposes some understanding of the entire field of archaeology—its major goals, relationship to other academic disciplines, basic interpretive concepts, and approaches to analysis of materials brought in from the field. In this introductory chapter these topics are addressed with specific concern for the way concepts, methods, and relationships affect data recovery.

The Nature and Goals of Archaeology

Archaeology is a field of study that seeks answers to questions about the nature of human culture and society as it existed in particular times in the past, and about cultural and social change. From the earliest presence of human life on earth, the products and by-products of human activity have accumulated on and in the ground. These traces provide a link to past lifeways and can reflect changes in behavioral patterns. Archaeology is the body of theory, method, and technique that guides the systematic recovery and analysis of the traces of past human activity. It enables scholars to bridge the gap between present and past cultures.

The discipline of archaeology rests upon two fundamental ideas. One principle suggests that human behavior modifies, transforms, or somehow reorganizes the natural world in ways that are distinctive of the activity involved. This may appear to be a trivial notion, for it seems obvious that human activity has a profound impact upon the world around us. Certainly this fact is inescapable in the modern world, since the production, consumption, and disposal practices of present-day industrial societies have almost totally remodeled the landscape. The simpler societies of the early stages of human cultural evolution have had a less pronounced impact, as have the nonagricultural societies of recent times. But whatever the period and whatever the scale of society, the record of human activity stands out from the record of general geological processes and of other forms of life. To the extent that the record is preserved and accessible for study, and to the extent that it contains distinctive behavioral signatures, archaeologists can "piece together the past," as the eminent prehistorian V. Gordon Childe has put it.

The second idea basic to archaeology is that it is possible to determine when a given event took place. Obviously it would be of little value to be able to identify archaeological patterns of human activity if it were not also possible to date them. The first attempts to apply dating techniques to the study of the past involved a "three age" system of relative dating, by which the archaeological deposits were arranged chronologically according to the presence, absence, or frequency of stone, bronze, and iron tools. This "three age" system was developed only after it was recognized that human behavior produced a distinctive, decipherable, physical trace (Daniel 1967). But accurate time-reckoning is far from obvious. Today, in addition to systems of relative dating which use distinctive materials or artifact styles to assign time periods, many methods have been developed in the physical sciences which permit precise determination of the absolute age of an archaeological deposit and the activity producing it. In this realm are such well-known methods as radiocarbon dating and potassium-argon dating.

It is often said that archaeology has three distinct but interrelated goals (Binford 1968; Dunnell 1978). One aim is the reconstruction of culture history. Pursuit of this goal begins with study of the age and geographic distributions of past cultures. By outlining the space-time relationships of cultures in a given region, area, continent, or the entire world, we can answer questions about the origins, achievements, and heritage of the various archaeological cultures. Additionally, comparative studies can be made of differing rates of cultural development and the interrelationships between regions. The second goal is the reconstruction of past lifeways. Here, the objective is to learn about the total way of life of a given archaeological culture. Although broad historical questions do have a place in cultural reconstruction, they are secondary to questions about such topics as social organization, economic activity, tool-making technology, religion, population size, health, and other aspects of the total fabric of everyday life. The third purpose of archaeology is the formulation of general laws of cultural change. Combining knowledge of culture history and the nature of individual cultures, an attempt is made to learn why cultures change, and in what directions. What explains the successes and failures of human cultures? Why have human populations come to dominate the animal world, and what is the future of mankind? Archaeologists who explore questions of this type are often referred to as "processual" archaeologists because they seek an understanding of the dynamics, or processes, of cultural change. This approach is often called *processual archaeology.*

If field projects were narrowly designed to explore the questions posed by only one of these approaches, exclusive of the others, important differences would be found in the kind of information sought and in the way field work is carried out. In culture-historical studies, for example, a premium would be placed on archaeological sites that had been occupied continuously, or repeatedly, over a long period of time. A sociocultural study aimed at elucidating the lifeways of an archaeological culture at a particular time would profit from the location of sites, such as dry caves or wet sites, in which normally perishable materials had been preserved. In the examination of a given site, a culture-historical study would primarily require trenching of the site to expose the sequence of deposits, while a sociocultural reconstruction study would require broad exposures to provide an outline of settlement layout. Probably the most distinguishing characteristic of a processually oriented project would be the need to acquire large numbers of sites of all kinds on a regional basis. Archaeological survey would play a more prominent role in a study of this type than it would in studies of culture history or past lifeways. The three approaches have other distinctive data requirements and field methods and techniques which will be clarified in later chapters. At this point, it should be emphasized that while specific questions entail specific field orientations, most archaeological research combines the exploration of a number of different kinds of questions.

The Academic Setting of Archaeology

In the one hundred or so years since its appearance in the western European intellectual tradition, archaeology has grown in complexity and taken a number of different directions. To a large extent it has maintained an independent identity, but it is usually found in close association with another discipline.

Archaeology's strongest relationship is with anthropology. In its focus on non-Western hunting-gathering and peasant societies, anthropology most often has been concerned with nonliterate peoples and cultures. Written documentation has been lacking or rare, and archaeology has been the primary source of evidence of these peoples' past. This relationship is exemplified in the Americas, and especially in the United States, where archaeology is viewed as a subdiscipline of anthropology. A common interest in human evolution and in the preliterate foundations of the world's great civilizations has also promoted a strong alliance between archaeology and anthropology. The biological development of the human species cannot be divorced from consideration of the development of culture, and studies of human fossils are necessarily carried out hand in hand with archaeological research. Along with an interest in human biological evolution, anthropology has delved into questions of cultural evolution, specifically, examining the complex, civilized societies of Mesopotamia, Egypt, India, China, Peru, and Mexico to learn how they developed from the humble village societies preceding them. Because the evidence for this development is in large measure archaeological, archaeologists have played a key role in exploring these and related questions.

Of equal importance to anthropology is comprehensive knowledge of the lifeways of past cultures. Since existing, or recent, cultures do not represent the total variability of cultural expression, it is necessary to turn to archaeology for comparative anthropological information on vanished societies. By the method of ethnographic analogy, the bare bones of archaeological evidence are fleshed out and extinct cultures may be added to the roster of known world cultures.

The anthropology-archaeology relationship in this case is a tightly interwoven one. The archaeologist depends on the anthropologist for detailed information about the relationship between ongoing behavior and the material products of that behavior, and the anthropologist, in turn, depends on the archaeologist for accurate reconstructions of past lifeways. This relationship has led to the emergence of a discipline known as anthropological archaeology, or ethnoarchaeology. In recent years, original field studies of hunting-gathering and peasant societies have been undertaken by archaeologists to determine precisely the archaeological signatures of various aspects of social organization and other facets of sociocultural behavior.

Archaeology also has close ties to history. The documentary record for many historical periods is impoverished or incomplete, and many branches of history are heavily dependent on the reports of archaeological investigation. Classical archaeology, for example, is a firmly established adjunct of studies in ancient history, and historical archaeology in the Americas plays an exceedingly important role in studies of the colonial history of the New World. Some facets of history, even in modern periods, are lacking in comprehensive or appropriate documentary records, and archaeology has made important contributions here also.

In recent years, in direct response to vigorous pursuit of questions about cultural process, archaeology has reached far beyond history and anthropology for interpretive tools. Particular interest has been shown, for example, in geographic models of settlement spacing, and recent archaeological literature includes many monographs and papers in which locational geography theory has been used to explain prehistoric site distributions.

Also, many archaeologists have borrowed extensively from ecological and evolutionary theory in the biological sciences in attempting to construct a theory of cultural change. At a higher level, general systems theory has been consulted frequently by archaeologists in a search for general principles of organizational change that might apply to human cultures.

Most of these explorations have been conducted by archaeologists who probably consider themselves most closely aligned with anthropology. As the search for appropriate explanatory principles widens, however, it becomes more difficult to view archaeology as bound to any particular discipline. The subject matter of archaeology is clearly different from that of disciplines which study the behavior of living people, a fact that distinguishes archaeology from the disciplines it serves. There is growing suspicion among a number of archaeologists today that the explanatory principles of cultural change may be as unique as the subject matter of archaeology—future generations may see the appearance of an archaeology which is more than a technical adjunct to established disciplines.

Whether functioning as a separate discipline or serving the aims of another, archaeology must have information about past environments, the ages of prehistoric events, and the condition and preservation of archaeological deposits. Were the vegetation and climate the same in the past as they are today? Of the plants and animals present in a given area in the past, which ones were selected for food and other purposes? What were the sources of materials used for tools and housing? For answers the archaeologist turns to botany, zoology, geology, mineralogy, and a host of other disciplines. In many cases the dating of archaeological deposits and the detection of archaeological remains require close cooperation between archaeologists, physicists, and chemists. Access to the theories of geology and soil science leads to an understanding of how an archaeological deposit came to have the properties observed by the archaeologist. While some archaeologists develop skills in these ancillary fields, most often it is professionals outside archaeology who perform the necessary analyses.

Archaeology and Science

Heated arguments have erupted in the last two decades over the nature of archaeology as a science. The debate has been given impetus by accusations by advocates of the processual approach, who contend that other approaches are not scientific. The literature contains numerous charges and countercharges. Some archaeologists who are oriented to the humanities have expressed the opinion that archaeology neither can, nor should, be scientific. But proponents of extreme opinions on either side must recognize the fact that archaeology is a heterogeneous field for which no single direction can be identified, and no single ethic forged. Some branches of archaeology clearly are not scientific, and need not be; others are scientific to the extent that they are objective, employ clearly defined terms, follow orderly, systematic, and logical procedures, and produce replicable results; still others may be fully scientific and generate predictions about the nature of human cultural change.

Because it is important to at least some kinds of archaeology, and because some of the topics introduced later in this text presume a position on the nature of scientific method, considerable space is devoted to a discussion of the basic components of scientific method. Figure 1.1 shows these concepts and their relations. Adapted from a model developed by Dubin (1969), the diagram may represent a unique view of how explanations are produced in science. In most respects, however, it is fairly nonpolemical and serves well as as a vehicle to introduce the use of scientific method in archaeology.

Definitions of theory abound in the literature of the social and natural sciences, but at the root of all definitions is the idea that, as the *Random House Dictionary of the English Language* expresses it, theory is "a coherent group of general propositions used as principles of explanation for a class of phenomena." Theory includes at least the following elements: a statement as to which part of the real world is relevant to a particular discipline, and a statement of the problem under investigation. In archaeology, it is the artificial characteristics of phenomena that are of particular interest. This does not mean that natural characteristics are ignored. To the contrary, knowledge of environmental context plays a key role in the evaluation of archaeological remains and in most if not all aspects of interpretation and explanation. Strictly speaking, however, if archaeological theory is to be regarded as separate from other theories, the principal concern is with the impact of human activity on a particular part of the world.

Several other elements of theory are noteworthy. Theory also includes classificatory units, explanatory concepts, laws, and assumptions. Classificatory units are conventional ways of organizing facts for the purposes of description and explanation. In archaeology, the *artifact type* is one of the most fundamental units. Explanatory concepts embody processes thought to be responsible for the distribution of the relevant facts of a disci-

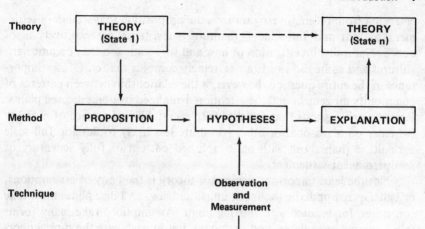

Figure 1.1. Model of scientific method. Propositions derived from theory are transformed into hypotheses by specification of techniques of observation and measurement. Explanation is achieved when the hypotheses are validated through repeated testing. Theory changes with the addition of new explanations.

pline, and in archaeology explanations include such terms as diffusion, invention, and migration. While the actual explanation in any given case will employ more specific concepts, these three processes are at the core of explanation in archaeology. They are in turn derived from the more inclusive concept of culture, which is discussed at greater length in a later section.

In theory, laws state the relationships between classes of facts and how change in one or more classes brings about changes in other classes. Laws crystallize the results of scientific work over generations of research. They have varying degrees of generality, and some may apply to the entire range of relevant phenomena while others may apply only to a small portion of it. In a purely formal sense they consist of a relational term linking two or more classes. For example, in the statement "family income and family status are positively related," the predicate indicates the value one of the subjects will have if the value of the other is known. The complete statement is a law, or more specifically, a law of interaction. Archaeologists have been hesitant to propose laws for cultural change, but one that seems to be emerging from recent investigations is the proposition that sedentary settlement pattern and full-scale agricultural subsistence are positively associated. Naturally, investigation of how and why some societies became agricultural and some did not is an extremely complex matter. Of key importance to the entire question, however, is the relationship between patterns of community movement and the attention demanded by domesticated plants. Recent work suggests that societies with an established pattern of mobility (whether on a seasonal or other basis) are less likely to develop full-scale agriculture than those with an established pattern of fully sedentary or semipermanent settlement.

Not the least important element of theory is the body of assumptions, or beliefs, that underlie the facts, units, and laws. All disciplines must take something for granted as a starting point. Assumptions take many forms (e.g., axioms, postulates, and premises), but in each case the most important characteristic of an assumption is that, although unproved, it may be regarded as practically beyond question. Also, in any attempt at explanation, a small number of assumptions is preferable, to keep the number of potential weak points in the explanation to a minimum.

Given the foregoing conception of theory, it should be apparent that explanation cannot be achieved without theory, or some of the components of theory, regardless of whether or not the theory is logically and coherently organized. Derogatory reference to theorizing and glorification of fact-finding, therefore, are nonsensical. Facts presuppose theory, and although it may not be immediately obvious, most investigations are motivated by an urge to explain something. Much of the recent writing about theory and archaeology has attempted at least to recognize this feature of theory and to urge that archaeologists make explicit the goals and methods of their research projects.

At the level of method in the diagram of scientific method in Figure 1.1, *propositions* are shown as deriving from *theory* and leading to *hypotheses* which in turn give way to *explanations*. Explanations are added to the fabric of theory, and accordingly the diagram shows theory changing as propositions are tested and explanations obtained. The diagram is meant to show the formal relationship between the basic elements of scientific method and at the same time illustrate the fact that theory is capable of change.

The terms proposition, hypothesis, and explanation are similar in meaning, and a few words on the differences between them are in order. A proposition is a statement about the relationship between classes of phenomena in which the values of the classes are specified. Within theory, for example, we may have a law which states that family income and family status are positively related. By adding values we have the proposition "families with low income have low social status." The concept of hypothesis refers to measurement of a controlled set of relevant phenomena with confirmation of the predicted values as specified in the proposition. Although corresponding in form to the proposition generating it, the hypothesis differs because it specifies how values are to be measured and how they are to be "filled in" with data. If a proposition can be shown to fit empirical reality through the test of a number of hypotheses and can be shown to obtain anywhere, anytime, the proposition is said to constitute an explanation. Insofar as an explanation produces new knowledge, it is incorporated in theory.

The observation and measurement of phenomena in reference to a problem result in the production of *data*. It is important to note, especially in archaeology, that data and phenomena are not synonymous. When we speak of *data recovery,* or *data collection,* we are not referring to the physical accumulation of the products and by-products of human activity. These things may be potential sources of data, but in and of themselves they do not constitute data. Data are not things, but rather categories of information embodied in things, and in the contexts and distributions of things.

If archaeological investigations are carried out in conformity with the model of scientific method presented here, where does field work, the subject of this book, fit in? Since field work is concerned with observation and measurement, it is a technical matter in reference to the model. If this book were concerned with a particular body of theory and method, we would of necessity have to speak of field techniques. This book, however, deals with field work independent of any particular problem, so a more general concept of method is implied. The field methods described here are general procedures leading to the production of data relevant to as yet unspecified problems.

The Concept of Culture

A comprehensive outline of the theoretical structure of archaeology is out of place in a text on field method, but at least one concept must be discussed, if only briefly. This is the concept of *culture*. It is important because of its basic role in the identification of relevant phenomena and in the interpretation of the archaeological record. The principle of culture probably underlies, in one way or another, most archaeological investigations, but it is most commonly acknowledged and consciously defined in anthropologically oriented archaeology.

In everyday usage, culture refers to etiquette, or to appreciation of the arts, but in anthropology the term has a special meaning. Here, culture refers to the rules of behavior widely held and commonly followed by the members of a community. For example, decisions about marriage partners are governed by cultural rules or norms. Parents have expectations about the type of person their children should marry, and they are hopeful, if not insistent, that the children share these expections. Passed from generation to generation, and within generations, cultural rules are the basis for individual action in most situations. Culture pertains to religious preferences, food choices, clothing styles, and the myriad other beliefs, values, and morals that guide us in maintaining our lives and in solving problems.

So much of human behavor is conditioned by cultural rules that the possession of culture has been said to constitute the single most important characteristic distinguishing humans from other animals. While genes are responsible for the transmission of many basic biological properties, most of the behavioral traits of humans are the result of postnatal cultural transmission. It is the flexibility of this manner of behavioral transmission, and the fact that lasting adjustments in behavior can be made within the lifetime of an individual, that underlie the enormous evolutionary sucess of the human species. Accordingly, it is not hard to understand why the idea of culture occupies a central position in the conceptual structure of both anthropology and archaeology.

In archaeology the concept of culture plays a critical role in the identification of phenomena which are the products of human behavior as well as in the interpretation of the archaeological record. Behavior guided by shared expectations often produces patterned distributions of archaeological remains. In other words, the repeated performance of some activity that results in a tangible, physical impact on the natural world will produce a structured association of phenomena. Recognition and formalization of this principle gave rise to modern archaeology. The detection and recovery of the patterned distributions of the tangible products and by-products of culturally organized human behavior are the goal of field work in archaeology.

At one time, the identification and listing of as many cultural norms as possible were principal objectives of archaeological interpretation. Recently it has been pointed out that this normative approach obscures individual variation. Cultural norms consist of a summary of numerous individual cases of activity conducted in the context of the norm. Few, if any, specific cases conform perfectly to the ideal, however, and many may represent radical departures. If one considers only the average, one will not obtain an accurate social picture of the degree of mastery of a skill, acceptance of a code of behavior, or the suitability of a rule to a particular situation.

For example, identification of irrigation as the predominant mode of agricultural practice in the prehistoric Southwest of the United States may serve to contrast that area with a neighboring one in which dry farming was of major importance. A normative characterization such as this, however, reveals little about the actual situation in which irrigation was just one of a number of agricultural systems. The Southwest is only marginally suited for agriculture, even with a mechanized technology, and investigation of the successes and failures of Southwestern prehistoric societies in establishing productive agriculture in this precarious environment requires a description of the full variety of agricultural systems. In both field work and interpretation, archaeologists must describe the total variation in the archaeological record in order to effectively pursue questions of human lifeways and cultural change.

The concept of culture has also played an important role in shaping one of the most important classificatory concepts in archaeology: the *archaeological culture,* or the *phase* as it is known in the Americas. The archaeological culture refers to a set of artifact assemblages in a continous space that exhibit a consistent association of distinctive stylistic elements. The organization of assemblages from a series of sites in a given region reflects an attempt to create an archaeological unit that corresponds to the idea of a particular culture in anthropology. Here, the total set of rules that guide behavior for a given group of people is said to be the culture, or phase, of that group. For example, the Issaquena Phase in the Lower Mississippi Valley, which dates from A.D. 500 to 700, is defined by a distinctive set of pottery types (Greengo 1964). It is assumed that the design elements which characterize the ceramics reflect a cohesive set of cultural practices extending to the aspects of life in the Lower Mississippi Valley at that time. While there are many objections to employing this concept in archaeology (Plog 1974), and many reasons why the anthropological and archaeological formulations of it are incompatible (Willey and Phillips 1958), nevertheless, it is an important factor in structuring analysis and, therefore, also significant in determining the nature of field work in archaeology. Most problems concerning culture history call for the location of field information that allows discrimination of distinct phases; sociocultural reconstruction leads field workers to sites with assemblages that will help describe as many cultural norms as can be inferred from archaeological traces.

The Concept of Artifact

It is often mistakenly assumed that culture alone is the subject matter of archaeology. Because this concept plays a central role in the identification and interpretation of archaeological remains, many archaeologists have, perhaps understandably, come to think that culture is the only thing they study. Culture, however, is an abstract notion that cannot be directly observed: to assert that it is the object of inquiry in archaeology is to commit the logical fallacy of misplaced concreteness. Archaeologists study the tangible products and by-products of human activity, which they assume reflect many features of human behavioral systems. The term *artifact* embodies this notion. The position taken in this book is that artifacts are the proper subject matter of archaeology and that location and observation of artifacts in their natural context are the objectives of archaeological field work.

While artifacts are often conceived in a narrow sense to refer mainly to manufactured utilitarian and ornamental objects, artifact is defined here in the broadest possible way in order to emphasize the comprehensive scope of archaeology. By considering an artifact to be any phenomenon whose properties are the result of human activity, we can include under the same term things as extensive and diffuse as the surface of the earth and as small and discrete as a tiny bead. This is consistent with the directions that archaeology has taken in recent years, since the scale of archaeological inquiry has expanded greatly to include the regional distributions and even the microscopic properties of archaeological remains. For example, trace element analysis of lithics is now common in studies of prehistoric technology; microscopic examination of tool edges and surfaces is considered essential in the study of tool function; soil samples collected from the pelvic areas of human skeletal remains are examined for traces of intestinal food waste; and microscopic grains of plant pollen are routinely collected and analyzed in an attempt to reconstruct prehistoric environments and climate. At the opposite extreme, archaeological remains from entire drainage systems and major environmental zones are being compared to study large-scale patterns of cultural adaptation. For adequate discussion of contemporary archaeological field work such a comprehensive definition of artifact is necessary.

A broad definition of artifact also serves as a constant reminder of the vast potential of the archaeological record to yield evidence of past human activity. Narrow, tactical definitions are necessary for the sucessful execution of a specific research design, but a field worker must not be confined by a narrow conception of the record. Especially in the early stages of an investigation, in poorly understood areas, it is essential that one be receptive to novel forms of the archaeological record. A broad definition of artifact can keep one alert to unanticipated sources of information.

Talking in general about artifacts, it is important to distinguish between *formal* attributes and *locational* attributes. Formal attributes consist of physical properties of phenomena such as color, mass, volume, length, width, texture, and weight. Archaeologically, physical analysis typically focuses upon such formal attributes as design elements, manufacturing scars, features related to tool use, and other attributes of style, function, and technology. The place where an item is found in space is referred to as its locational attribute. The major purpose of archaeological field work is not only to locate artifacts, but to record their locations as well. In addition to boxes and bags of broken or complete tools and implements, manufacturing by-products, bone, soil, charcoal, and pollen samples, an archaeological project typically generates reams of notes, dozens of maps, and hundreds of photographs. These records contain figures, written commentary, and illustrations of the locations of everything that was found. Without precise information about their locations, collected items are useless for interpreting or explaining the past.

The Spatial Organization of Society

Human groups are complex phenomena that display a variety of organizational forms in the number and distribution of their constituent members. A great deal of this organizational variety is expressed in spatial distributions of human activity, and consequently archaeological analysis places a premium on knowledge of the horizontal distribution of artifacts and the archaeological sites themselves. Two systems of spatial division found commonly in archaeological work are summarized below. They are analytic units which condition archaeologists' perceptions of the archaeological record and thus are of considerable interest in any treatment of recovery method. Discussion of them in this introductory chapter is important because they represent formal and scale differences in the archaeological record and also imply differences in field recovery.

In a midcentury synthesis of the theory and method of American archaeology, Willey and Phillips (1958:18-21) identified four spatial divisions as important in archaeology. The smallest of these is the *site,* defined as a fairly continuous distribution of the remains of a former single unit of settlement. A somewhat larger division is the *locality,* which is a "geographical space small enough to permit the working assumption of complete cultural homogeneity at any given time." The *region* is a geographical space of a size that might be occupied by a "social unit larger than the community" and that corresponds generally to a distinct physiographic subdivision. The *area* is the largest unit in this system and denotes a region, such as the American Southwest, that corresponds to a major physiographic province. Exact size is not specified for any of the units because they are conceived as relative to the landscape of a particular area and to the scale of the society under investigation.

An update of spatial concepts in archaeology is found in the divisions outlined by Flannery (1976:5-6). Like the Willey and Phillips system, this synthesis of concepts has been employed widely in recent years, but its divisions are directly related to study of the Mesoamerican village. At the lowest level is the *activity area,* which is defined as a "single locus of activity of one or more members of a community." House floors make up the next unit of important spatial organization, and the floors themselves may be composed of several activity areas and nonportable features. A *household cluster* includes a single house and the features and activity areas surrounding it. In Mesoamerica, villages typically display patterned arrangements of houses, and Flannery's system consequently includes two levels of organization between the household cluster and the village. One is the *courtyard group,* which consists of several houses sharing a common patio. At a higher level is the *barrio,* defined as "related courtyard groups whose architecture, material remains, and other attributes may distinguish them from neighboring barrios."

Beyond the village level are several other levels of interaction that have figured prominently in recent archaeological investigations. One of these is the *catchment area,* which is conceived as the zone of food and material resources within reasonable walking distance of a settlement. Groups of settlements and their catchment areas commonly are interrelated in larger systems of interaction, on a regional scale, that often correspond to drainage systems. Regions themselves are integrated through trade exchange systems to produce an even higher level of interaction and a larger scale of spatial organization.

It should be evident that for the most part the systems outlined by Willey and Phillips and by Flannery overlap. The lack of correspondence that occurs in the lower levels of organization can be attributed to differences in the general situations each system is designed to investigate. The Willey and Phillips scheme focuses on investigation of problems of culture history. Consequently it places greater emphasis on the higher levels of interaction. Although concerned with the internal structure of individual sites and with the kind of human organization represented by different classes of sites, the culture-historical approach emphasizes the historical events affecting a site. Analysis centers on the identification of the major events represented by an occupation, or sequence of occupations, and upon the integration of events in a number of sites to produce local, regional, and area chronologies of history. The Flannery system, in contrast, reflects modern concern with intrasite structure and specific information on the organization of human activity within sites in order to characterize sociocultural reconstruction and processual orientations. The more refined spatial divisions, below the level of site itself, draw attention to information about task differentiation, group size, group hierarchies, and other aspects of social organization necessary for studies of this type. Even at levels above the site division (although a correspondence is seen between the two) each system has a different emphasis. The Willey and Phillips system concentrates on units of chronological synthesis, and the Flannery system stresses units of social interaction.

Summary

Archaeology is a scientific discipline that addresses questions about human culture history, past lifeways, and the processes of cultural change. It is founded upon the notions that many aspects of human behavior produce distinctive physical traces, and that it is possible to determine the time at which those traces were produced. Closely allied in many ways with anthropology and history, archaeology has associations with many disciplines and has recently shown signs of developing an independent body of theory.

Two concepts fundamental to archaeology, whatever its goals or relationship with other disciplines, are the ideas of *culture* and *artifact*. Culture refers to the rules of behavior that guide the actions of the members of society. It is this patterned behavior that on the one hand enables the identification of archaeological phenomena and on the other hand provides the basis for the interpretation or explanation of those phenomena. While it is normative at one level, the concept recognizes that the behavior of individuals and groups displays considerable variation from the norm. The job of the archaeologist is to observe and record this variation.

An artifact is any phenomenon whose properties are the result of human activity. Including microscopic qualities and regional distributions of the products of past human activity, this concept identifies the subject matter of archaeology and emphasizes the vast potential of the archaeological record to yield evidence of past human behavior. Like the concept of culture, the concept of artifact, as defined here, serves a general orienting function.

A number of spatial divisions of the archaeological record have been devised by archaeologists to enable study of the organizational aspects of past human societies. Housing units and associated facilities, groups of household units, entire settlements, and local and regional distributions of settlements reveal some of the complex organizational characteristics of human groups. Investigation of the structure and function of past human groups, and of the web of interaction between groups, depends upon the development of a series of spatial divisions of archaeological distributions.

Discussion of the goals of archaeology and its place in the academic setting, along with the basic principles of scientific method and of archaeological interpretation and explanation, provides the necessary background for any treatment of archaeological field method and technique. Field work does not take place in a vacuum; it cannot, and should not, be undertaken in isolation from the comprehensive discipline of archaeology. The objectives of any particular field expedition are directly related to the theory and method of the discipline as a whole.

Chapter 2

The Archaeological Record and its Formation

Because the products and by-products of human behavior vary so greatly, it is important to discuss some of the forms that the archaeological record can take before we describe methods and techniques of field recovery. In this chapter, a general conception of the archaeological record is presented along with detailed consideration of various kinds of clustered artifacts and a discussion of nonclustered remains. The chapter closes with a brief treatment of some aspects of the formation of the archaeological record. This topic is of special interest because it is becoming increasingly apparent that interpretation and explanation of the record must take into account any processes that may mask the relationship between the record and the behavior producing it.

Apart from the general concept and specific characteristics and forms of the archaeological record, it should be noted that we are concerned with a contemporary phenomenon. The human behavior that produced the record, whether remote in time or close to the present, remains part of the past. Furthermore, in the time intervening between the record's initial formation and the present, various cultural and noncultural processes have acted upon it to mask or obscure its relation to human behavior. Ignorance of this fact, or failure to acknowledge it, has led to many naive conclusions about past behavior (Schiffer 1972). Some of the perspectives that have been developed to cope with this fact are described in a later section of this chapter.

Another general comment to be made about the archaeological record concerns the fact that, in contrast to written documents, it is unbiased by human motives. It is possible to "falsify history" through the written record, but it would be a rare thing indeed if people intentionally set out to create an archaeological record that reflected behavior as they wanted it to be viewed by later generations. This fact is what makes archaeology such a potentially powerful tool for understanding the past, in both prehistoric and historic periods.

Concept of the Archaeological Record

In keeping with the general definition of the proper subject matter of archaeology advanced in the preceding chapter, it is helpful to conceive of the archaeological record as a more or less continuous distribution of artifacts over the land surface, with highly variable density. At one time, the record was more narrowly conceived to include principally, if not exclusively, artifacts that occurred only in dense concentrations. Certainly it was known that isolated artifacts could be found outside clusters, but research problems of the day singled out clusters as the most relevant part of the record. The advent of regionally oriented research programs, specifically those designed to investigate questions of cultural process, has enlarged the scope of archaeological field work, and it is apparent today that a broader concept is necessary. Casual observation shows, and field evidence proves, that just as the activities of individuals and communities take place over broad expanses of the landscape, the archaeological products of those activities are also widespread. In fact, it is exceptional to find an area which does *not* contain artifacts, and even in reports of field studies restricted to locating and recording dense clusters, investigators often ruefully note that determination of exactly where clusters begin and end is a serious practical problem.

While a distinction between clustered and nonclustered artifacts appears to be important in the history of archaeological field research, at least in the Americas, it is difficult to give precise meaning to these density-related terms. Ideally, the distinction is meant to separate artifacts that are the product of human activity concentrated in a particular place (clusters) from artifacts that represent diffuse activities (nonclusters). However, it is not possible to assign values of universal application to these terms. The reason is that the scale of society under investigation has an important effect on what is perceived as clustered and what is not. Thus, for example, what appears to be clustered in the archaeological record of hunting-gathering societies may be considered nonclustered in the record of complex societies. Precise definition of these terms, therefore, is an operational matter and is done in the context of a particular study.

The archaeological record is defined here as a *land surface* phenomenon because although a large part of it exists below the surface, its thickness is insignificant in geological terms. Certain kinds of archaeological sites consist of layer upon layer of accumulated deposits, which in some cases reach several hundred feet thick. Sites of this nature are exceptional, however, and for the most part the record is thin and close topresent-day surface level. While biased in favor of surface-exposed and thin deposits, the definition can encompass most subsurface deposits, even those of some depth.

The archaeological record is traditionally said to consist of three kinds of artifacts: cultural items, cultural features, and ecofacts (Binford 1964). *Cultural items* are discrete entities whose formal or locational properties are the product of human activity. In this class are tools, ornaments, building materials, and the by-products of manufacturing and construction activities. Also included are natural materials called *manuports*—objects which have been removed from their original positions and used in some way without altering their formal properties (e.g., river cobbles brought to a settlement and used to weigh down the margin of a skin dwelling cover).

Cultural features are clusters of cultural items that as a group constitute a meaningful association. Pits, burials, structure foundations, hearths, and concentrations of manufacturing debris or food processing waste material are examples of this kind of artifact. With a similar meaning, but employed when the patterned association of culturally relevant items has reached a massive scale, is the term *fragile pattern.* This term was coined to refer to trail patterns that are visible as slight depressions and altered arrangements of rocks on the generally smooth desert soil in the American Southwest (Hayden 1965), and could also apply to roads, field systems, and water control devices (e.g., irrigation canals).

Ecofacts are materials such as fossil pollen from plants that were used for food or other purposes, fossil human feces (*coprolites*), animal bone, and other humanly produced residues that may shed light on dietary patterns, food-getting and food-processing strategies, and other aspects of the articulation of cultural systems with the natural environment. Often referred to as nonartifactual remains because they do not usually exhibit attributes of deliberate manufacture or use, ecofacts have come to play an increasingly important role in archaeological studies.

This general division of the archaeological record is significant in the analysis of past cultural systems. It also determines artifact recovery in the field. Cultural items can be removed from their archaeological context for subsequent analysis in a laboratory. But cultural features, because their properties are not inextricably bound together, cannot be removed from their context without significant loss of information. The observation and recording of features must be done in the field. Ecofacts include both discrete items (such as butchered animal bones) and nondiscrete features (such as soils enriched by fats and proteins as a result of food processing) and thus may be either transported to a laboratory for analysis or observed and analyzed in the field.

An accurate description of the archaeological record in any given region should include information on the following five general properties to be complete: artifact variety, artifact quantity, the clarity of the record, the integrity of the record, and the environmental context of artifacts (Glassow 1977). *Variety* refers to the different kinds of archaeological materials that occur in a region. Do cultural items consist largely of stone artifacts, or do shell and bone tools and debris, and items of other materials, occur as well? What kinds of features are most commonly encountered in the region? *Quantity* refers to the numerical frequency of the remains of a region. Which kinds of artifacts are abundant and which are rare? What are the density characteristics of the various kinds of items, features, and ecofacts?

Clarity refers to the degree to which archaeological resources may be isolated from their contexts. This property reflects the ability to distinguish on a horizontal plane between the products of successive occupations, and on a vertical plane between distinct episodes of deposition or accumulation. Put in another way, clarity is concerned with the degree of mixing that has taken place which might blur the distinctions between discrete activity events.

Integrity is a property of the archaeological record concerned with the degree of preservation represented by a given deposit. Chemical decay and mechanical alteration take a heavy toll on the material products of human activity, and a given deposit may show, from one end to the other, or from top to bottom, different stages of disintegration. Items of different materials are preserved in differing degrees, and items of the same material varying in size and shape are affected differently by breakage and dislocation. Furthermore, many deposits have suffered postdepositional disturbance or truncation; this also is an aspect of the integrity of the record.

Lastly, the *environmental context* of artifacts is an essential property of the archaeological record. The selection of a place for the conduct of some kind of behavior can be influenced in a general way, or in a very specific way, by the nature of the surrounding environment. No archaeological field description is complete without the inclusion of information on such aspects of the natural environment as topography, proximity to water, soil group, soil drainage characteristics, and locally available raw materials.

Clustered Artifacts: The Archaeological Site

As noted above, it is common in archaeology to distinguish between clustered and nonclustered archaeological remains. In this section some of the variety that exists in the former is surveyed. The term *archaeological site* as used here is synonymous with *cluster* since, although some authors have suggested that a site can be "as small as the spot where an arrowhead lies" (Hole and Heizer 1973:111), the concept most often applies to dense concentrations. Thomas (1975:63) has noted that the more inclusive usage, while unassailable in principle, is cumbersome in practice. In fact, reported sites in most cases consist of locations that contain a substantial number of items or features, usually with high density characteristics.

Within the class of archaeological remains that are labeled archaeological sites, considerable variation in size and composition exists. For the earliest periods of prehistory, sites may comprise only thinly scattered remains of several hundred chipped stone tool fragments and manufacturing waste products, often accompanied by bones of animals and humans. This debris accumulated in the camps of groups numbering approximately 25 individuals who seldom occupied more than several hundred square meters. With the appearance of urban communities, sites achieve massive proportions and cover many square miles. The ruins of monumental architecture and complex dwelling units are highly visible indicators of the location of such sites.

Sites vary also in relation to the land forms they occupy. Deposits at the mouth of a cave or under a rock overhang (rock shelter) are considered *closed sites*. Located in confined land forms, the deposits are quite deep and often contain a layered record of thousands of years of occupation. Closed sites are notable because of the layering, but also because they are protected locations which favor preservation of artifacts that normally would perish. Rock shelters in the western American deserts, for example, are almost completely protected from water and often contain basketry, wooden tools, and mummified human burials. Ordinarily, even in highly arid environments, such materials would perish in open situations.

Open sites are located on unconfined landforms, such as meadows, low hills, and valley floodplains and terraces. If there were no social or natural barriers to restrict the expansion of settlements located on these landforms, the archaeological deposits of open sites tended to spread out rather than build up. This is not to say that open sites never exhibit layers like closed sites. In fact, many of the deepest stratified sites are in open terrain. For example, floodplain settlements that must be abandoned annually as flood waters inundate a valley commonly attain a layered quality. The St. Albans Site (Broyles 1971) in West Virginia is 11 meters (36 feet) deep with 40 distinct layers, and the Koster Site (Struever and Carlson 1977) in Illinois is 9 meters (30 feet) deep with 12 layers. The layers in both sites represent seasonal occupation by hunting-gathering peoples of the Archaic Period in the eastern United States and date between 8000 and 1000 years B.C.

Another way of talking about sites is to note whether they are restricted to the surface or whether they extend below the surface. If the majority or all of the individual items that make up a site are scattered on the surface and digging into the ground produces few or no artifacts, the deposit is a *surface* site. Probably most surface sites occur because the sediments on which they developed have been blown away by wind. Lightweight soil particles are removed by this deflation process, but the heavy items, including tools and bones, remain. This erosion is most common in desert and arctic areas where vegetation is thin and wind velocity high.

Many sites are found on landforms that at the time of occupation, and later, were unaffected by wind and water erosion or affected only slightly by these and other geologic and soil-forming processes. The artifacts comprising such sites escape burial and remain completely or partially exposed from the moment of discard or loss. Hilltops and broad plains often contain surface sites for this reason. In forested areas, surfaces sites may be obscured by leaves, shrubs, and flowering plants. Forest clearance for agricultural purposes has brought thousands of such sites to light.

Sites that consist largely or completely of buried deposits are called *subsurface* sites. Subsurface sites may contain archaeological features such as fire pits, post molds, compacted-dirt house floors, and food waste. They also frequently contain layered deposits, and this allows the development of cultural chronology. Layering, or *stratification,* is discussed later.

Subsurface sites that consist of items, features, and residues in the exact location of the activities producing them, or only slightly altered from their original location, are referred to as *primary* sites. Sites composed of materials that have been totally dislocated from their original positions are referred to as *secondary* sites. The clearest example of a secondary site is a case in which floodwater has washed away an archaeological deposit. House patterns, pits, burials, and all other features are destroyed. Only the durable, discrete objects are preserved and these are transported downstream and relocated in a new position. In their secondary location, they are more a geological deposit than an archaeological deposit, since the distribution pattern of individual objects is a result of periodic flooding rather than human activity.

While primary sites naturally are the basic sources of archaeological data, secondary sites are not completely devoid of information and for some periods of time may constitute the major body of evidence about past human activity. The Old World Lower Paleolithic, a period between approximately two million and 500,000 years ago, is a case in point. Only about ten sites are known for this important beginning episode in human prehistory. Known primary sites include Terra Amata in France, Isimila in Tanzania, Kalambo Falls in Zambia, Torralba-Ambrona in Spain, and Olduvai Gorge in Kenya. Although thousands of tools dating from this period have been recovered archaeologically, by far the largest number are found in the gravel of ancient streambeds. One prominent reason for the rarity of primary Paleolithic sites is age. Destructive forces have been acting for a longer time on these early deposits than on more recent sites. Additionally, human groups of this period do not appear to have frequented geologically protected landforms such as caves and rock shelters. Most early settlements were in the open and thus more susceptible to destruction. While information on the structure and function of early human groups cannot be obtained from the Lower Paleolithic secondary sites, it is at least possible to obtain an approximate picture of regional cultural differences and of changes in style and technology from the contents of these dislocated assemblages.

Up to this point sites have been classified according to their physical characteristics. Sites may also be differentiated on the basis of the kind of activity they represent, as when we speak of a *kill site* or a *ceremonial site*. Another basis for distinction is the quality of life and types of activities in settlements, as reflected in terms such as *city* and *village*. Just as the modern world has its resort towns, mining towns, monasteries, mineral quarries, farm towns, capital cities, county seats and the like, the ancient world had a great diversity of settlements.

The settlement pattern of the semisedimentary, hunting-gathering, and fishing cultures of the Late Period (1500 B.C. to A.D. 1800) in the Columbia Plateau of eastern Washington (Nelson 1973) illustrates the wide variety of sites that can result from activity differentiation. The floodplain of the Columbia River was a focus of settlement and activity, although the semidesert terrain and coniferous forests of the hinterland were also utilized. Winters were icy and cold, and groups of 100 to 150 people sheltered themselves in groups of semisubterranean log and sod houses clustered at well-protected places along the Columbia River. The winter villages were vacated at the end of winter when warm temperatures permitted the erection of less confining, portable wickiuplike dwellings. In late spring, the groups divided into family units and most people moved for a month or so into the hills to dig tuberous plants. These roots were roasted and steamed in special pitovens at base camps. In late summer and early fall, people reassembled on the banks of the Columbia, often in very large numbers, to take advantage of salmon traveling upstream to spawning grounds in mountain headwaters of the Columbia. The large fishing camps, usually located at narrow constrictions, falls, or rapids, have a distinctive archaeological character. Roots and fish were dried and stored in pits and other containers constructed in rock shelters near a family's winter village. Rock shelters were also used by hunting groups as temporary camps and frequently served the additional function of a place to bury the dead. Burial was often made in the loose debris of rock slides at the base of canyon walls and in other open locations.

Such a diversity of sites in the Late Period of the Columbia Plateau is not unusual for prehistoric cultures. Activities were varied in the past as in the present, although differences in the Lower Paleolithic probably were fewer than in more recent periods. Similarly, hunting-gathering, early agricultural, and urbanized cultures show many kinds of site variation. Whatever the stage of economic and cultural development, however, site diversity is commonplace in the archaeological record and of special interest in archaeological interpretation. The impulse to describe sites in terms of the dominant activity producing them is a natural and analytically important procedure.

A common and salient characteristic of subsurface sites is *stratification*. As artifacts and soils accumulate at a given spot, the resulting deposit may attain a layered appearance. Layering, or stratification, will be most

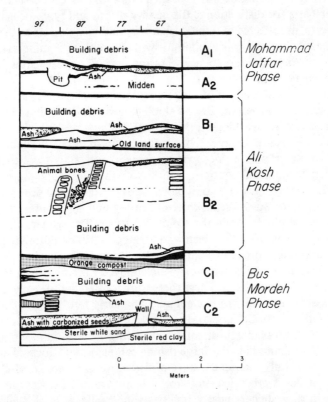

Figure 2.1. Statigraphic profile from Tepe Ali Kosh, Iran. Strata A1 through C2 represent distinct episodes in the vertical growth of this Neolithic village. The strata have been assigned to the cultural phases shown on the right margin of the diagram. (From ''Prehistoric and human ecology of the Deh Luran Plain,'' by Frank Hole et al., Figure 8. In *Memoirs of the Museum of Anthropology,* No. 1. Ann Arbor: University of Michigan. 1969.)

striking when materials of sharply different character alternately pile up in the same place. For example, where coastal hunting-gathering people who included shellfish in their diet discarded shells on the bank of an annually flooding river, a stratified deposit of alternating river sand, silt, and shell results. The same effect can be seen in our city streets when repair work requires trenching through the roadbed. In older parts of a town, the wall of a repair trench may reveal traces of an early corduroy road overlain by cobbles, then bricks, and finally asphalt. Although composed entirely of artificial or arranged natural materials, stratification is exemplified here just as much as in the riverbank example. Figures 2.1 and 2.2 show drawings of stratification in two well-known archaeological sites.

Stratification is important archaeologically because of the geological principle known as the Law of Superposition, which states that, in a given sequence of layers, the bottom layer is older than the top layer. This principle can be used to determine the relative ages of a number of sites, but in order for it to be useful in dating, sites must have at least two prominent layers of cultural debris. In fact, subsurface deposits with a single layer of artifacts are often said to be *unstratified* archaeologically because alone they cannot be correlated with other sites to form a dated sequence. For this reason, sites with multiple strata are most valuable to archaeologists.

Nonclustered Artifacts

Although sites traditionally have received the greatest attention from archaeologists, sites are not the only source of information about past lifestyles and historical change. In fact, one might argue that emphasis on sites produces a lopsided view of the past. Much of our lives is spent in settlements, it is true, but most of the materials and foods that equip us and sustain us come from the hills, mountains, fields, and plains of the wider landscape. The artifacts lost or discarded in agricultural pursuits, in hunting, in mining raw materials, and in acquiring the many plants, animals, and minerals upon which we depend are an essential part of the archaeological record.

A hypothetical example of a modern farmstead will emphasize the importance of nonclustered artifacts. A farm would, upon abandonment or destruction, result in a fairly substantial archaeological site. Assuming excellent preservation, it would not be difficult to identify the chicken coop, main house, hog pen, garage, barn, workshop, and other typical structures of a farmyard. This is because distinctive tools and refuse are associated with each kind of structure, and because the sizes, shapes, materials, and

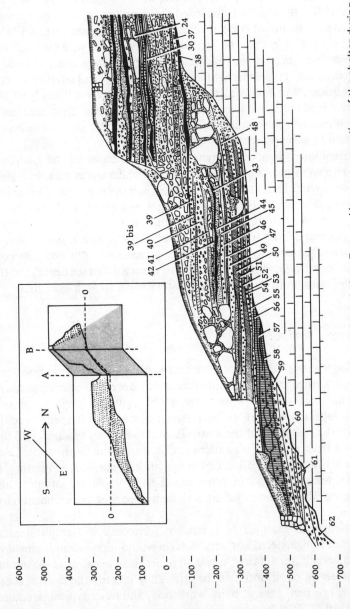

Figure 2.2. Stratigraphic profile of the Combe-Grenal Rockshelter, France. Human occupation of the shelter during the Middle Paleolithic added artifacts to the strata which formed by geological processes as sediments were blown in from outside and rock fragments fell from the roof (not shown in the diagram) to the floor of the shelter. (From Bordes 1972).

constructional features of the structures also are unique. In addition, work areas outside specific structures also are an important part of a farmyard and involve a unique set of assorted artifacts. Study of the organizational aspects of the farmyard from a social point of view would be possible with this type of data. Knowledge of agricultural methods and techniques could be gained by examination of the barn with its remains of cultivating tools, such as plows, harrows, discs, and hoes, and seeds of the plants that were cultivated. Barns, however, are storage facilities, and questions about farming methods would be answered only partially, if at all, from the barn's contents. The most direct source of information about cultivation practices will be found in the fields where the crops were grown and harvested. Plow furrows, broken tool fragments, associated soils, chemical traces of fertilizers, and other isolated and diffuse artifacts should provide an accurate picture of farming methods. Although difficult to find, such evidence repays the effort of field work many times over.

Two archaeological studies in which nonclustered artifacts have been used to study prehistoric hunting patterns illustrate the potential of this aspect of the archaeological record. Both studies were based on the distribution of *projectile points*, which are defined as pointed, generally symmetrical objects with some means of hafting provided at the base. This artifact class is referred to by a neutral term rather than by a term such as arrowhead or spear point, because the specific type of weapon represented is difficult to infer from the size, shape, weight, or other formal attributes of the points. In many parts of the Americas, stone-tipped projectiles were a popular weapon both in the hunt and in war, and projectile points chipped or ground to shape are a common archaeological find. Points also represent a style of artistic expression and so are important archaeologically as a means of reconstructing local and regional community boundaries, and of estimating the ages of archaeological sites.

One interpretation that can be made with projectile points concerns whether hunting was practiced singly or in group parties. Points found in the remains of settlements, however, are of little use for this type of reconstruction. Like the hypothetical farmyard example, the best source of information on hunting practice will be the specimens found in the environment where they were used. The two studies summarized below made a special effort to obtain this type of information. They illustrate the interpretive potential of stray artifacts.

In the Lower Illinois River Valley, Luchterhand (1970) spent one month examining the artifact collections of several lay archaeologists who had accumulated thousands of specimens from an area of about 700 square miles over a period of about 35 years. Luchterhand was interested in Early

Archaic Period (8000 to 5500 B.C.) hunting patterns and selected from the collections approximately 300 points that date to that period. Few if any of the points were from known sites; they occurred singly or in small groups in otherwise barren fields.

Upon selecting his sample, measuring the points, and noting point locations, Luchterhand studied the distribution of the points in relation to landform zones of the Illinois River Valley. The environment consists of a wide area of flood-deposited bottomland bordered by high, eroding bluffs and flat, expansive upland prairie. Early Archaic projectile point styles occurred in all zones but were heavily concentrated in narrow valleys between the bluffs. This pattern is thought to indicate the hunting of white-tailed deer, which today congregate during the winter months in these valleys. Deep snow and rough terrain would make deer easy prey in December, January, and February, and they probably were the major food of Archaic people in the difficult winter season.

A similar study was conducted by Dancey (1974) with data from the semidesert eastern region of the state of Washington. In order to collect information on prehistoric utilization of upland landforms, long narrow survey transects measuring hundreds of meters long were projected across the terrain. Projectile points were the most common artifacts in the transects, and most of the 40 points found were broken in ways that clearly indicate a poorly aimed projectile that struck ground rather than an animal. Plotted in relation to local habitats, the points concentrated in depressions along the ridges that are a prominent landform of the area.

Several interpretations may explain this distribution. The depressions, or saddles, as they are called locally, may have served to funnel deer or similar game into ambush. Game browsing on shrubs in the canyons might have been driven up the gulleys leading to the saddles, and then through the saddles into a cross fire of arrows. Alternatively, saddles may have been attractive resting places for deer, where they could be caught off guard by skilled hunters. Saddles offer protection from the wind and are shady at times of the day when the rest of the area bears the full intensity of the sun unfiltered by clouds. Modern deer can be found resting in saddles during the early morning hours, and contemporary hunters typically follow the ridges. Prehistoric hunters may have done the same.

Formation Processes

Not long ago, a prominent American archaeologist coined the phrase "Pompeii mentality." This refers to the mistaken idea that all archaeological sites are as well preserved as the site of Pompeii, a large part of which was covered by mud and ashes from the eruption of Vesuvius. So sudden was the catastrophe that many citizens of the city had no time to flee— people and artifacts in Pompeii were captured in time. A similar situation was recently discovered and is currently under investigation at the Ozette Site of the tip of the Olympic peninsula on the coast of the state of Washington (Daugherty and Kirk 1976). Here a number of wooden plank houses of prehistoric Makah Indians were flattened by a landslide of mud from the bluffs towering behind the settlement. Excavation has uncovered household items exactly as they were stored before the slide. The inhabitants of these houses must have had better luck or more advance warning than the Pompeiians, for no skeletons have yet been reported.

Sites like Pompeii and Ozette are rare. The more common archaeological site has suffered thousands of years of disturbance of one kind or another and presents anything but a clear picture of prehistoric life. Erosion washes away all but the most compact sediments. The wind relentlessly lifts lightweight dirt particles and carries them away. Soil acids corrode metals, dissolve inorganic materials, and erase stratigraphic boundaries, and organic material is devoured by acids and bacteria. Earthworms imperceptibly but pervasively churn the earth and destroy or displace the subtler archaeological features. And it must not be forgotten that cultural processes also disrupt the record, for example when rebuilding requires the leveling of old structures and new constructions dig into old deposits. The concept of *entropy* describes the tendency of the material world to deteriorate toward uniformity. Archaeological deposits suffer progressive disintegration as much as any other earthly phenomena.

Robert Ascher was one of the first archaeologists to argue that inferences about past human behavior require information about the changes that take place in the archaeological record from the original accumulation or deposition of artifacts up to the time they are observed in the present. In a provocative and pacesetting article (Ascher 1968) that drew examples from his research on a modern junkyard and a contemporary Seri Indian community in Sonora, Mexico, Ascher distinguished between inhabited, ghost, and archaeological phases in the formation of the archaeological record. In the inhabited phase, the accumulating material products of human behavior suffer disorganization largely as a result of the recycling of serviceable material. Additionally, observation of the Seri community over time showed that while distinct, clear spatial clustering of households and associated debris was present in the newer sections of the settlement, in the older sections these distinctions were obscured. As a result of both recycling and decomposition, the record was being blurred into and blended with the natural sediments. Often efforts to arrest disorganizational changes are made in the inhabited phase, as when the dead are buried in specially prepared graves or tombs. Following abandonment of a community, in the ghost phase, Ascher noted that dissolution is almost exclusively a function of natural processes of decay and breakage. Natural disorganization may also in some cases be slowed, or arrested, by events such as burial by volcanic ash and pumice. Archaeological investigation itself introduces a new phase of disorganization "because contexts . . . are not predictable, and awareness of them may postdate their destruction" (Ascher 1968:46). Ascher (1968:52) concludes that "since the connection between the archaeological present and the ethnographic past lies along the route of increasing disorder, the advancement of interpretation depends on knowing what happens along that route."

In a more recent treatment of formation processes, Daniels (1972) constructed a model of the origin of archaeological information (see Fig. 2.3) in which special attention was given to the control of postdepositional factors (Ascher's ghost phase) and research factors (Ascher's archaeological phase). From an original potential population of artifacts in use in a human group, certain artifacts are deposited and preserved to form the archaeological record which may subsequently be sampled by archaeologists who record and publish the results of their investigation. By and large, the factors affecting the deposited artifact population are uncontrollable, but allowances can be made for them. This entails the formulation of hypotheses that account for the horizontal and vertical distribution of artifacts by purely noncultural processes. Can the frequencies of artifacts of different materials (e.g., stone, bone, shell, and wood) from site to site, or within a site, be ascribed to corresponding differences in the preservative qualities of the soil? Do the items found together in different strata of a site reflect contemporary deposition, or has differential postdepositional movement by size brought about a spurious association? It cannot be emphasized too strongly that although the aim of archaeological investigation is to produce data that will lead to an understanding of the cultural past, steps must be taken to acquire information bearing on natural processes that obscure or bias the record.

Along with Ascher, Daniels stresses that beyond the cultural and natural processes affecting it, the archaeological record suffers further deterioration at the hands of the very people who wish to use it to understand past human behavior. His discussion of research factors entering into the production of archaeological data identifies location of investigatory units, recovery procedures, artifact processing and analysis, and reporting as the major points in research where a potential for distortion exists. An

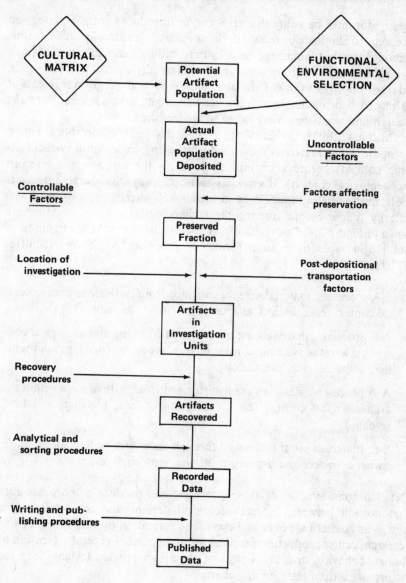

Figure 2.3. A model of the causation of archaeological data. Descriptions of the archaeological record are blurred reflections of the cultural matrix in which artifacts are produced. Factors such as preservation and postdepositional transportation are uncontrollable while those related to data recovery, analysis, and publication can be controlled. (Adapted from Daniels 1972)

investigator must be aware that error can be introduced at these points and take steps to eliminate or reduce it. Some control measures include rigorous methodology, the planned redundancy in recording, randomization of tasks both in the field and in the laboratory, and quality control of observation and recording. The utility of archaeological reports about given segments of the record depends on knowing what biases and errors entered into the research and what steps were taken to control them.

Michael Schiffer (1972; 1976; 1977) has devoted considerable attention to ways in which materials move through the ongoing cultural system (systemic context) before accumulating to form the archaeological record (archaeological context). His models of the pathways that durable elements (tools, machines, and facilities) and consumable elements (foods and fuels) typically follow before entering the archaeological context as refuse are shown in Figure 2.4. One result of his research has been the formulation of four major types of cultural formation processes, as follows (Schiffer 1977:16-17):

1. S-A processes: materials are transformed from systemic to archaeological context (e.g., discard, abandonment, loss, and disposal of the dead).

2. A-S processes: materials are transformed from the archaeological context back to the systemic context (e.g., scavenging, collecting, pothunting, archaeological excavation).

3. A-A processes: materials are transformed from state to state within the archaeological context (e.g., excavation of pits, plowing, and land leveling).

4. S-S: materials are transformed through successive system states, (e.g., owner transfers and deposit in shrines, museums, or libraries).

Detailed consideration of these processes can produce a more accurate "connection between the archaeological present and the ethnographic past," as Ascher expresses it. Beyond the formation process aspect of this research, refuse production practices are an important general dimension of human behavior, and knowledge of them can provide insights into the nature of cultural stability and change.

In the postdepositional context, the archaeological record is distorted by a multitude of biological, geological, climatological, and soil-forming processes. A complete listing and description of them would be tedious here. Some of the major natural processes that result in the mixing of materials in soil, or in item associations that may potentially be misinter-

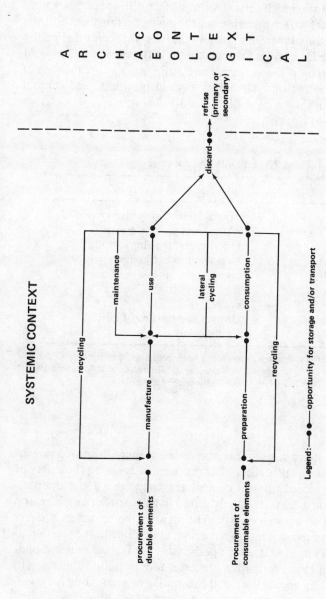

SYSTEMIC CONTEXT

ARCHAEOLOGICAL CONTEXT

refuse (primary or secondary)

discard

recycling

maintenance

use

lateral cycling

consumption

manufacture

preparation

recycling

procurement of durable elements

Procurement of consumable elements

Legend: ●—— opportunity for storage and/or transport

Figure 2.4. A model of durable and consumable element pathways in the systemic context. Before discard and incorporation into the archaeological context as refuse, durable and consumable elements undergo a series of transformations in the living community. In simplified form, the model shows the pathways these elements take from the point of raw material procurement to the point at which they become refuse. (Adapted from Schiffer 1972)

preted as the product of past human behavior, are given in Table 2.1. In addition to these factors, which pertain to subsurface disturbances, are non-cultural processes that affect materials on the surface subsequent to their deposition or accumulation. Such factors include the consumption by animals of select portions of food refuse and the differential weathering of surface-exposed materials. Once again, the distribution and frequencies of cultural items can be radically altered by natural processes, and cultural inferences drawn from them must filter out the distortion.

Table 2.1. Soil Mixing Processes

Process	Soil-Mixing Vectors
Faunalturbation	Animals (burrowing forms especially)
Floralturbation	Plants (root growth, treefall)
Cryoturbation	Freezing and thawing
Graviturbation	Mass wasting (solifluction, creep)
Argilliturbation	Swelling and shrinking of clays
Aeroturbation	Gas, air, wind
Aquaturbation	Water
Crystalturbation	Growth and wasting of salts
Seismiturbation	Earthquakes

From "A Survey of Disturbance Processes in Archaeological Site Formation," by W. R. Wood and D. L. Johnson, in *Advances in Archaeological Method and Theory,* vol. 1, pp. 315-383 (New York: Academic Press, 1978).

In conclusion, it might seem that acknowledgment of the processes that can distort the archaeological record has cast serious doubt on the ability of the archaeological record to yield dependable knowledge about the past. Skeptics of archaeological method might find in these studies ample reason to discount the value of archaeology. The view of the record as a *direct* reflection of past behavior seems to have been undermined. The reaction to these studies, however, should not be pessimism, but instead renewed optimism, since recognition of formation processes adds a realistic dimension to archaeology. Knowing about them, and controlling or accounting for them, can lead to strengthened, not weakened, conclusions about prehistoric cultural patterns and the dynamics of cultural change. As understanding of distortion factors advances, the credibility of archaeology will increase.

Summary

The archaeological record is conceived as a more or less continuous distribution of artifacts over the land surface with highly variable density characteristics. The record consists of cultural items, cultural features, and ecofacts, which in some instances are clustered in space and in other cases are nonclustered. The clusters are most ofter referred to as archaeological sites and traditionally have received the greatest attention in archaeological research. Nonclustered artifacts, along with low-density clusters, have taken on greater importance in recent years with the emergence of regional studies, which emphasize the recovery of information concerning comprehensive subsistence, settlement, and land use patterns. The accurate, complete description of the archaeologial record in any given area necessarily includes consideration of artifact variety and quantity, the clarity and integrity of the record, and the environmental context of the artifacts composing it.

Archaeological sites vary in size and composition, and in relation to the landforms on or in which they are located. Another variable is whether they are restricted to the surface or whether they extend below surface. Subsurface sites consisting of artifacts in their original location are referred to as *primary* sites, while sites whose artifacts have been removed from their original locations are referred to as *secondary* sites. Primary sites are of greatest importance in archaeology, but secondary sites can provide useful information of a limited sort. One of the dimensions of compositional variation in archaeological sites stems from the primary activity, or activities, producing them. The variety of functions represented by a set of sites from a given period make up the settlement pattern of the prehistoric population under investigation. Finally, subsurface sites differ in the number of layers they contain. Single-layered deposits are referred to as *unstratified* sites while those containing multiple layers of cultural deposits are termed *stratified* sites. The latter are extremely important in developing relative chronologies for a region.

Many artifacts do not exist in clusters, but instead are widely spaced on the landscape. Items lost or discarded at the location or near the location of hunting, gathering, or food-producing activities frequently do not form clusters, and though difficult to locate, they can prove a valuable source of direct information on subsistence practices and land use.

Archaeological deposits suffer progressive disorganization through time as a result of many cultural and natural processes. Geological, biological, and chemical processes act in countless ways to deteriorate the archaeological record. Human activity also has a disruptive effect. A number of studies of these processes have suggested that cultural activities (such as recycling, broadcasting, and blurring) and postdepositional natural processes (such as frost heaving, animal burrowing, and differential weathering), along with the disturbing effects of the research process itself, must be understood before an adequate grasp of the archaeological record can be achieved. Consideration of these transformation processes can lead us beyond a naive perspective, in which the record is viewed as a direct reflection of past human activity, to a more realistic one which recognizes and attempts to control and understand the many disruptive factors.

Chapter 3

Research Design in Field Archaeology

Early in the history of archaeology, investigators entered the field with a general notion of their objectives and adopted *ad hoc* artifact recovery strategies. Recently it has become common, if not necessary, to conduct research according to carefully constructed research designs. The design is formulated before field work begins, and outlines, at the very least, a theoretical basis for the proposed research, implications of previous research, specific hypotheses to be tested, test implications of the hypotheses, and techniques of data collection and analysis (Raab 1977:168-70). Developing a research design compels an investigator to think through the project from beginning to end and to clearly establish the means to accomplish the objectives of the work. When research is performed with an explicit plan it is guaranteed to be more successful than that done by a "seat-of-the-pants" approach.

In this chapter research design is carried from the initial stage of problem formation up to the end of a field project when data for the solution of the problem is created. Later steps, concerned with the analysis of field data and the actual solution of the problem, are obviously beyond the scope of this text. This discussion offers a general model of data recovery for prehistory developed by Dunnell and Dancey (1979). The major elements of this model and their interrelationships are shown in Figure 3.1.

The general model may be summarized briefly before each element is considered in detail. Beginning with the formulation of the research problem which is objectified as one or several hypotheses, a geographic area is selected that is known or expected to contain relevant data. Because it is neither possible nor necessary to examine all parts of the area in a field program, a sampling strategy is drawn up to provide an explicit, rational basis for selective coverage. In order to locate the sampling units indicated by the sampling strategy, and to provide a framework for recording artifact locations, it is necessary to have already adopted an ap-

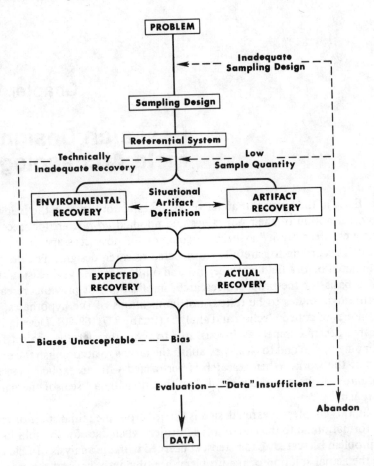

Figure 3.1. A model of data recovery for prehistory. The major elements of research design are shown in relation to the formulation of a problem and the production of data. All or portions of a field investigation must be redone if the initial recovery project contains unacceptable biases or if the data are insufficient for solution of the problem.

propriate referential system. An operational definition of artifact tailored to the specific conditions of the area must also be devised as part of the recovery design. Artifact and environmental recovery is performed according to appropriate methods and techniques; then the actual product of the field work is compared with the expected results to assess the degree of success of the recovery program. The difference between expected and actual recovery is termed *bias*. If biases are minimal or nonexistent (a rare occurrence), the results are evaluated to determine whether they provide sufficient data for the solution of the problem. A positive evaluation means that enough data has been produced; a negative one that some aspects of the design must be modified and additional field work performed.

Problem Formulation

A fundamental tenet of our industrial society is that work runs more smoothly and efficiently and output is higher when the purpose of a project is carefully spelled out. This tenet applies to most scientific research, including archaeology. In business and industry, the purpose is to turn out a project, or render a service. In science the purpose is to add to knowledge. The careful formulation of the questions stimulating research in archaeology can prevent or reduce the aimless collection of irrelevant facts.

A statement of the purpose of research has a far-reaching impact on an entire project. It tells where to work, at what times of the year, and for how long. It determines how much of an area must be inspected and the degree of thoroughness required. It specifies the kinds of artifacts that are sought and in what quantity. In short, the problem to be investigated conditions nearly all aspects of field work: the more carefully the problem is conceived, the more efficient and productive the field program will be.

In the development of a research problem, attention is given to at least four factors. First of all, it must be established that the problem addresses a question, or set of related questions whose answers will make an important contribution to knowledge. Thus, it may be argued that the research attacks an issue that is of major concern in the discipline and one that has not been resolved in the existing literature. If the research proposes to answer questions that are marginal, or even completely outside the range of interests current in the discipline, it must be shown that, while initially they may seem anachronistic, in the long run the answers will provide a new perspective on existing problems or will lead to a reformulation of the research direction of the discipline. Justification of the research problem is a necessary ingredient in scientific research.

The second factor in the development of a research problem is to define the nature of the question and to determine its expression. A research project should address a specific, clearly stated question, and not just a general topic or area, or set of data (Plog 1974:18-25). A question as specific as "Why did horticulturalists living on the Colorado Plateau about A.D. 700 begin to develop water control techniques?" is a legitimate research problem, whereas broad questions such as "What is the nature of cultural change in the Colorado Plateau?" or "What kinds of archaeological remains are present in the Colorado Plateau?" are not. The answer to the specific question will contribute to understanding of culture change, and provide information on the range of remains in an area, but topical or data questions are not sufficient starting points for the design of scientific research.

In addition to justifying the problem, and formulating it in specific, clearly stated terms, it must be decided whether or not the question is answerable. The third factor in problem formulation is establishing that the problem can actually be solved. In archaeology it is not uncommon to find examples of field research aimed at discovering the precise location of the first domesticated form of some plant or animal, the first occurrence of a technique, or the first social unit in which a major organizational change occurred. Innovations usually represent minor, accidental deviations from a preexisting pattern and their traces are archaeologically undetectable (Flannery 1969:85). If, for example, we were to ask with respect to the previous question about the Colorado Plateau, "What site contains evidence of the initial attempts at water control?" we would be asking an unanswerable question. The nature of the information base of a discipline limits and places constraints on the kinds of questions that can be addressed.

The final factor in problem formulation concerns how the terms of the problem are conceived. Here, the researcher must make certain that the question is phrased in objective terms. In the preceding example, if it is impossible to define "horticulturalists" and "water control techniques" in ways that allow identification of the archaeological manifestations of these phenomena in the research area, the problem is not objectively stated. Since the results of research must be shown to apply to a concrete body of information, it is necessary from the outset to make certain that the questions pertain to measurable phenomena. If this cannot be done, subjectivity enters into field observations, and research is destined to fail from the start.

Besides reviewing archaeological literature, it is important to make a study of the natural and social environment, and history, of the projected study area. Information must be compiled on local bedrock geology, and plant and animal ecology. Current geological processes, such as flooding and erosion, should be understood. Although difficult, one should try to determine how the modern environment differs from the prehistoric setting. At the same time the history of current land use practices should be researched. Has the land been extensively drained? Have prominent features been leveled and water courses diked or dammed? Familiarity with all cultural and natural features of the area of investigation and an evaluation of formation processes (see Chapter 2) are necessary for the identification of relevant environmental variables. These factors affect the preservation, condition, and visibility of the archaeological record and determine the design of a sampling program.

In areas colonized by Western industrialized societies, anthropological reports or travelers' accounts of the previous inhabitants are useful sources of background information. In the Americas, for example, most archaeological research is related to Native American, or Indian, prehistory. In many cases survivors of Native American village and tribal groups were visited shortly after first contact by anthropologists who recorded details of the precontact way of life. Such reports are called *ethnographies* and contain information on village location, tool technology, and many other facets of history and life. Archaeological studies in the Americas often begin with the location of ethnographically reported settlements and work backward in time from the known to the unknown, carefully piecing together Native American prehistory. This research strategy is known as the *direct historical* approach.

Closely related to problem formulation, and proceeding hand-in-hand with it, is the construction of one or several hypotheses to express possible solutions to the problem. In constructing hypotheses, the researcher turns to the theoretical literature of the discipline for a set of laws and propositions that seem appropriate to the problem. Alternatively, a body of theory might be constructed specifically for the research at hand. (The nature and relationship of theory and hypothesis are discussed in Chapter 1.)

Most commonly, hypothesis construction follows the method of devising multiple working hypotheses (Chamberlin 1965). By this method a number of reasonable answers are conceived, including contradictory ones. Consider the question, "How did the prehistoric hunting-gathering populations of a given region organize their exploitation of plant and animal foods?" The answer might contain one of several possibilities. The settlement/subsistence systems of these cultures may be related to the microenvironmental structure of plant and animal communities, or to the availability of water and other materials necessary for food processing, or to distance from major permanent settlements, or to the cycle of ceremonial events.

Designing a field project to collect data relevant to several hypotheses has at least two benefits. First, the hypothesis selected as the answer to the original question is strengthened by comparison with other hypotheses which do not give a solution. Secondly, single solutions are rare, so multiple working hypotheses can show how a number of factors are interrelated. In the hypothetical example, the settlement/subsistence system may be influenced predominantly by the microenvironmental distribution of plants and animals, but also by the ceremonial cycle and by raw material availability. A single hypothesis, therefore, more often than not produces an unsatisfying and simplistic answer.

A simple example illustrating the interplay between problem formulation and field research can be found in the research of J. G. D. Clark (1954, 1972) at Star Carr, England. This site (Fig. 3.2), excavated by Clark between 1949 and 1953, represents a temporary encampment at the edge of a lake approximately 9500 years ago. The settlement covered a small area and may have been occupied during midwinter and spring. Abundant faunal remains of deer and fowl suggest a hunting orientation for the inhabitants at that time of year. Given the small size of the camp, the group occupying it cannot have included more than four or five families. For years Clark had been

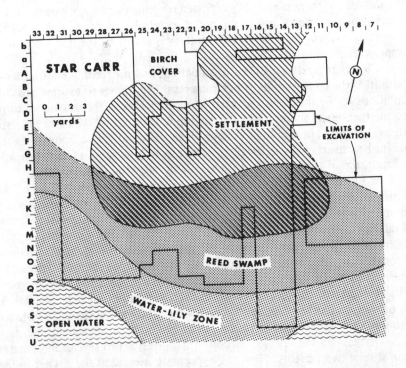

Figure 3.2. The Mesolithic site of Star Carr, England. Reconstruction of the settlement area and the local environment concluded that Star Carr was a seasonal encampment on the edge of a lake. The excavation grid is shown along the margins of the diagram. (Adapted from Clark 1954)

interested in the western extension of an early Mesolithic cultural tradition termed Maglemosian (8000 to 5000 B.C.) Evidence of this culture was most abundant in Denmark and other countries of northern Europe, but stray finds had turned up periodically at various localities in northern Britain. The British finds raised questions about the western boundary of the Maglemosian culture province. During this era, the British Isles were joined to the mainland due to lowered sea levels. If a Maglemosian settlement in primary condition could be found, the question of distribution might be answered.

In addition to a primary site, Clark sought archaeological data that would allow reconstruction of the lifeways of Maglemosian culture in Britain. In his own words:

It was appreciated that the need was no longer to excavate and classify flint implements or rely on fortuitous discoveries of loose objects of antler or bone, but to investigate a site yielding direct information about the way of life of Maglemosian Man and about the character of his immediate environment. This . . . was most likely to be achieved by excavating in waterlogged deposits, either in a bog settlement or immediately contiguous to a settlement on dry land, since here alone were the physical conditions necessary for the survival of a broad range of organic materials likely to exist in this part of the world. (Clark 1954:xxi.)

By maintaining contact with local observers and collectors, Clark learned of Star Carr. During a visit to the site he determined that it promised to satisfy the dual conditions of his problem. Flint tools from excavations in the site by a local collector were comparable to Maglemosian implements found on the continent. The major concentration of artifacts occurred approximately one meter (3 feet) below the surface, contained in a deposit of peat and organic mud. Using volunteer labor and arranging for pumps to keep the pits dry, Clark recovered abundant perishable items of bone, antler, and wood. Notable among the finds was a birch tree apparently felled to stabilize the marshy lakeshore on which the camp was originally located. Also of note, a wooden paddle was found. Besides these items, other tools and preserved bones from food waste enabled Clark to reconstruct the site occupants' use of the surrounding territory, aspects of their social, intellectual, and religious life, and many other social features.

Another example of problem-oriented research is provided by the work of Richard MacNeish for the R. S. Peabody Foundation (MacNeish 1964; Byers 1967). MacNeish concentrated on the origins of New World maize agriculture. His ultimate goal is to determine the social consequences of the shift from food collecting to food production and the effect of highly productive maize crops on the development of sedentary settlement and urbanism. The key to understanding these processes is discovery of where and when maize was first domesticated and incorporated in the human diet. In planning his research, MacNeish reasoned that he should look in areas in which wild varieties of maize-related grass are found. This decision narrowed the search to Mexico, which in prehistoric times had the densest New World populations, and was the center of maize production. The field was further narrowed to arid areas within Mexico because they have the greatest potential for botanical preservation. Within the arid area, field work concentrated on rock shelters, since they are the driest spots in a desert and frequently contain stratified deposits.

After years of work at various localities in Mexico, MacNeish was led to the Tehuacan Valley in the state of Pueblo, southeast of Mexico City. This valley was chosen because research in southern and northern Mexico, though producing examples of early maize, failed to disclose corn remains resembling a hypothetical wild form of the plant. The discovery of 60,000-year-old fossil corn pollen in the Mexico City area suggested the high, dry central portion (the Mesa Centrale) of Mexico as the place of origin. The Tehuacan Valley is in this highland area. Over a period of four years, more than 300 open sites and rock shelters were located in the Tehuacan Valley and either surface-collected or excavated. In Coxcatlan Cave, MacNeish found what he was looking for. In the lower levels of the deposit, dating to approximately 5000 B.C., tiny, inch-long preserved cobs of an extremely primitive form of maize were found. At the time these finds represented the earliest known maize in the Americas. The discovery suggested that the Tehuacan Valley was an appropriate region for investigation of the processes of domestication and the social effects of food production.

MacNeish's work on the origins of maize domestication illustrates elementary hypothesis formulation. When asking where maize was first domesticated in the Americas, MacNeish hypothesized that the origins of maize would be found in the desert regions of the Mesa Centrale. In a more complex way, Flannery (1968) proposed an explanation of how the process of domestication occurred. With direct reference to the Tehuacan Valley, he constructed a hypothesis which states that hunting and gathering peoples dependent on seasonally recurring natural foods systematically schedule which of several available foods will be harvested at a given season. The key to the scheduling process is relative abundance, the more numerous plants or animals being selected over less abundant ones.

According to Flannery, this scheduled harvest of grasses with edible seeds led to genetic change among the wild maize population. The direction taken by the evolving maize placed it higher and higher on the list of scheduling priorities. Gradually, the feedback between the human and plant populations resulted in domesticated maize and semisedentary human groups. In order to test this hypothesis, data on settlement pattern, ecological zones, and a complete array of economic plant and animal remains are required for each period of occupation. The question is a complicated one, as is the hypothesis, and they require complex field data.

An illustration of multiple working hypotheses is found in the work of the Southwest Anthropological Research Group (SARG 1974). This research consortium has developed a working relationship among more than 30 archaeologists all over the United States. The regional focus of this enterprise is the American Southwest. SARG members are unified in pursuit of a broadly conceived common problem, that of explaining variability in the area's settlement distribution through time and space. Why sites are located where they are found archaeologically is a basic problem that can be incorporated into various research designs without radically altering the objectives of the member archaeologists. Three hypotheses have been advanced (SARG 1974:11):

1. Sites were located with respect to critical on-site resources.
2. Sites were located so as to minimize the effort expended in acquiring required quantities of critical resources.
3. Sites were located so as to minimize the cost of resources and information flow among sites occupied by interacting populations.

It should be obvious that these statements do not conform to the more precise concept of a hypothesis presented in Chapter 1. However, it can be seen that an attempt has been made in these initial stages of research to identify several different variables that might account for the distribution of archaeological sites in the research area.

With the problem formulated and hypotheses constructed, the research design process moves to the stage of putting the hypotheses into operation. This stage includes the adoption of a sampling design, provision for a referential system, objective definition of the information base, and decisions about appropriate recovery methods and techniques. At this point the investigator is concerned with the structure and execution of the recovery program. The following sections discuss each of these elements of research design in turn.

Sampling Design

Rarely is it possible, or even desirable, to achieve total coverage of a region or site. A choice must be made of which parts to favor and which to exclude. One alternative is to make the choice on a purposive basis. Intuition or prior knowledge of archaeological remains in an area may suggest ways of defining the sampling space. These approaches will produce results, to be sure, but artifact proportions and distributions may be distorted by unconscious biases. In place of purposive selection, many archaeologists have turned to *probability sampling.*

The virtue of probability sampling is that choices are randomized. Depending on the method used, and there are many, the items or units of the site or region are given statistically determined chances of being included in or excluded from the sample. Randomization is important because it permits predictable statements about a total population of artifacts or sites based on the sample. Thus it is not unlike election polling whereby a small fraction of the electorate is questioned to ascertain the voting preferences of the whole.

The differences between purposive and probability sampling can best be understood by looking at a single site which has been investigated using both approaches. Test excavation of DcRu2 on Vancouver Island near Victoria, British Columbia, was performed in 1972 by nonrandom sampling, and in 1973 using random sampling (Spurling 1976). The site is a beachside shell midden with no surface features. It covers approximately 4200 square meters (5040 square yards) and is estimated to have been occupied between A.D. 1200 and the time of European contact (approximately A.D. 1800). As shown in Figure 3.3, the 1972 excavation consists of a series of trenches located near the beach, on the east side of the site. The trench locations were selected on the basis of judgmental criteria. Fundamentally, these criteria included proximity to an eroding portion of the midden and open space in which to work. Approximately 35 cubic meters of sediments were excavated.

Selection of excavation units in the 1973 season at DcRu2 was guided by a simple random sampling design. The locations of the 1973 test squares are shown in Figure 3.3. In contrast to the clustered trenches of the 1972 season, the 1973 units are widely dispersed over the site. The selection process involved determination of the site perimeter, mapping the site, gridding it in units 2 meters (6.5 feet) square, and numbering the units. Target units were chosen by consulting a table of random numbers. The sample size (0.76 percent by volume of the entire site) was made to approximate the sample obtained in the previous season.

The DcRu2 probability sampling design is an instance of sampling where the population under investigation is unknown. The excavator was interested in the characteristics of tools, features, strata, and other cultural and natural material. But these things were buried, and they could not be sampled directly. Instead, the site was gridded and the units of the grid were

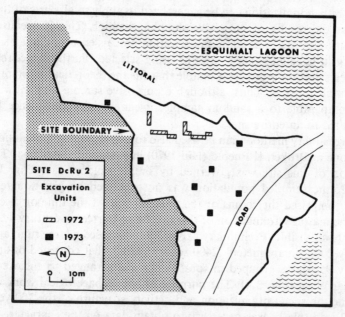

Figure 3.3. Site map of DcRu2, Vancouver Island, British Columbia. The site was tested in 1972 with a series of trenches placed in the site on a nonrandom basis. The site was tested again in 1973 using a random sampling design for excavation unit placement. (Adapted from Spurling 1976)

sampled. Since each grid unit had an equal chance of being chosen, the field worker's intuitive or convenience-oriented preference for one part of the site over another was prevented. It is known that communities at all stages of social complexity exhibit internal functional differentiation. Randomized selection of archaeological investigation units helps to ensure that this variability is represented in the recovered sample.

The DcRu2 sampling design illustrates another important property of probability sampling—the ability to extrapolate with confidence from the sample to the population being sampled. Comparing the two seasons, and thus two strategies, it was found that the two samples did not differ in any significant way. The proportions of tools, including bone, antler, and stone implements, found during both seasons were approximately the same in both samples. The correspondence is either accidental or the result of an unusually homogeneous site. Even if the sample had been different, random sampling has an advantage over purposive sampling since the results obtained by randomization can be generalized to apply to all parts of the site, whereas the results of purposive sampling cannot. This is because randomization of the excavation unit selection process ensures that all squares in the grid have an equal chance of being selected. Furthermore, the randomized selection produces a sample that fits the theoretical assumption of inferential statistics. Thus, although a purposive sample may show variation comparable to a random sample, it cannot with confidence be extrapolated to an entire site.

Probability methods can be used also to sample known populations, as was done at Broken K Pueblo (Hill 1970) in east-central Arizona. The excavation of this site was governed by simple random sampling. Unlike DcRu2, the sampled population was not obtained by grid squares, but rather comprised the rooms of the pueblo ruin. At the time of discovery, only the masonry foundation of this twelfth to thirteenth century A.D. settlement was visible. Preliminary exploration disclosed a large ruin, approximately 2000 square meters (2400 square yards), that consisted of approximately 95 rooms grouped in four blocks and arranged to enclose a rectangular plaza (Fig. 3.4). The purpose of the archaeological work was to examine the social organization and activity structure of the 700-year-old ruin. To do this, it was necessary to obtain data on the characteristics of rooms and their contents.

Time and money restrictions prevented complete excavation of the pueblo, and so it was decided that work would be limited to a 50 percent sample. The excavators felt this sample would suffice to achieve a balanced picture of all facets of the social system of the group that inhabited the pueblo for 100 years or more. In order to obtain the desired representative sample, all rooms were numbered and a table of random numbers was consulted to determine which ones to excavate and in what order. The sample selected (see Fig. 3.4) provided an unbiased spatial distribution and an unbiased selection of room sizes.

The original 50 percent of 46 rooms was supplemented by 8 additional rooms selected on a judgmental basis. Together the 54 rooms produced 2931 tools, 26,060 potsherds, 9999 animal bones, 570 plant seeds, and 115 pollen samples (Hill 1970:12-14). Analysis of these data suggests that the rooms had been used principally for habitation, storage, and ceremonial purposes. Individual households appear to have performed nearly all functions necessary to their day-to-day, year-to-year existence. The data indicate a lack of centralized economic or political authority. The clustering of design elements of pottery suggests, however, that households were aligned according to kinship relationships. Two basic clusters of similar design elements and five secondary clusters were present. The original report of the work at

BROKEN K PUEBLO

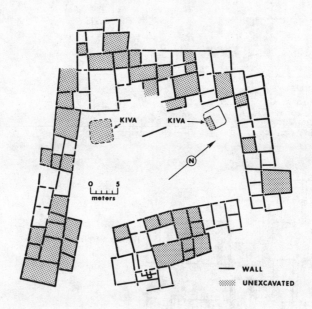

Figure 3.4. Site map of Broken K Pueblo, Arizona. The excavated rooms in this prehistoric settlement were selected on a random basis. (Adapted from Hill 1968)

Broken K suggests that these may correspond to the clan and lineage respectively, which is the social organization common among present-day puebloan communities (Hill 1970:108).

The examples of probability sampling as used at DcRu2 and Broken K Pueblo illustrate single site applications. Sampling can be used also to implement regional investigations, as was done in a recent project in the Chaco Canyon National Monument, New Mexico. In this investigation, a 52-square-kilometer portion (20 square miles) of the canyon was chosen as a test of the ability of several regional probability designs to produce a consistent, significant, and reliable picture of the region's archaeological sites (Judge, Ebert, and Hitchcock 1975). The region had been intensively examined in several previous seasons and a map was made of the 1130 archaeological sites found in the region. The test used four different techniques, combining quadrat (square) and transect (rectangular) units with systematic and simple random techniques of unit selection and placement (see Fig. 3.5).

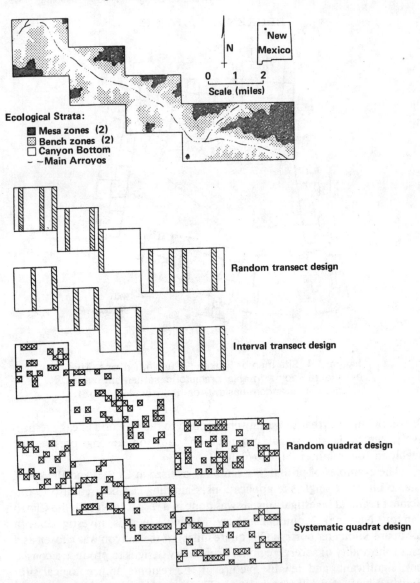

Ecological Strata:
- ■ Mesa zones (2)
- ▨ Bench zones (2)
- □ Canyon Bottom
- – –Main Arroyos

Random transect design

Interval transect design

Random quadrat design

Systematic quadrat design

Figure 3.5. Sampling strategies for an investigation of the Chaco Canyon National Monument, New Mexico. Each of the four strategies shown represents a twenty percent sample, divided by ecozone, of the portion of the canyon shown at the top of the figure. Each strategy produces a different distribution of sampling units within which intensive survey was conducted. (Reproduced from Judge et al. 1975 by permission of The University of Arizona Press.)

The major conclusion of the Chaco Canyon test was that different designs are useful for different purposes. Overall, however, judging the designs in terms of precision and accuracy, interval transects were found to give the best estimation of site distributional characteristics, followed by random transects, random quadrats, and systematic quadrats, in that order.

While site locations were known beforehand in Chaco Canyon, this test illustrates how various designs can be applied to sampling unknown populations of sites. Once again, the use of probability over purposive designs has the advantage of producing data that can be interpreted by inferential, probability-based statistics.

Although sampling designs are still at an elementary stage there is little doubt that they have an important part to play in archaeology. As interest in regions increases and as sample sizes get larger, prehistorians must turn to probability theory to help maintain objectivity in the selection of samples and to lend statistical credibility to conclusions derived from study of these samples.

Referential Systems

Control of space is essential to obtain information on the distributional characteristics of archaeological phenomena. This control is achieved through the acquisition or creation of maps at scales that can accommodate the placement of sampling units in the field and the recording of artifact locations within these units. Maps provide the point of reference for the controlled study of spatial variation in past cultural systems. Attention must be given in the early stages of research to the kinds of maps available commercially and the preparations needed for new mapping in the field. The establishment of benchmarks, the identification of field monuments, or the location of existing survey datums that serve to identify the relationship of the map to the land surface is also necessary.

Two kinds of maps are used in archaeology: regional maps and sampling unit maps. In studies where the site itself is the unit of investigation, a sampling unit map is used. Regional maps at convenient scales are available commercially from private and governmental sources. In the United States, maps in the National Topographic Map Series published by the U.S. Geological Survey (Geological Survey 1969) are ideal for archaeological purposes (see Fig. 3.6). The large-scale (1:24,000) series is particularly useful for general planning purposes and for establishing sampling unit locations. Approximately 22 by 27 inches in size, the individual sheets in this series can be folded or rolled to take into the field. Marginal tick-marks

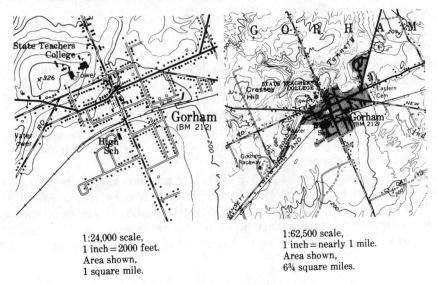

1:24,000 scale,
1 inch = 2000 feet.
Area shown,
1 square mile.

1:62,500 scale,
1 inch = nearly 1 mile.
Area shown,
6¾ square miles.

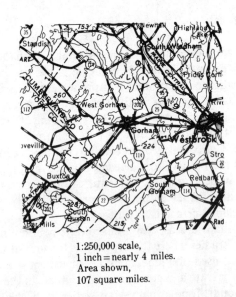

1:250,000 scale,
1 inch = nearly 4 miles.
Area shown,
107 square miles.

Figure 3.6. Three common map scales. These illustrations from large-scale (1:24,000), medium-scale (1:62,500), and small-scale (1:250,000) maps in the U.S. Geological Survey National Topographic Map Series show how detail is reduced as the map scale becomes smaller.

at uniform intervals of latitude and longitude permit the location and recording of unit corners according to a universally accepted system of spatial reference. Recent editions also contain marginal marks in the Universal Transverse Mercator (UTM) system (described in Chapter 5) which has become popular among archaeologists.

Commercial maps are available for most areas and an archaeologist is rarely required to commission a regional mapping survey or to perform the job personally. However, specific locations within a region usually are not mapped at scales large enough for archeaological work, and so practical knowledge of surveying principles, equipment, and techniques is a necessary part of field training. Within sampling units it is particularly important to have maps at a scale allowing clear illustration of item and feature locations, smaller collection and recording units, as well as the contour of the surface at an interval that shows significant relief.

Among the instruments most commonly used by archaeologists in making maps and in locating points on preexisting maps are compasses, transits, and alidades. The simplest and least expensive is the hand-held *compass* such as the Silva Ranger which uses a mirror to simultaneously sight a point and read its compass direction. The compass housing in this model is set in a rectangular, translucent plastic base plate which has ruled edges and permits the transfer of readings to a map. Although the accuracy of some hand-held compasses is claimed to be as high as one-half or even one-sixth the true directional reading (bearing or azimuth), for the most part the compass is less accurate than other instruments. In spite of low accuracy, its low cost, lightweight compact design, trouble-free mechanisms, and easily understood and executed procedures make the compass a highly useful surveying and mapping instrument.

Another surveying and mapping instrument commonly used in archaeology is the *transit*. This instrument consists of a revolving telescope mounted on a compass dial. The optical properties of the telescope and the calibrations of the compass dial are designed to display readings that are within seconds of true bearing. The precision attainable by the transit makes it very useful for mapping sampling units that contain abundant, dense archaeological items and architectural features.

The *alidade* is an instrument well suited to mapping the surface contours of sampling units, along with the locations of small collection and recording units within master units. The alidade is a telescope mounted on a rectangular plate, the edges of which are parallel to the line of sight. It is used with a *plane-table* on which a piece of drawing paper is fastened. The plane-table and alidade combination has an important advantage over the transit and related instruments (e.g., the theodolite, which measures angles). While transit survey observations must be recorded in a notebook and plotted later in a lab to compile the final map, alidade measurements can be transferred directly to the sheet of paper on the plane-table to produce a finished map in the field.

The purchase or rental costs, portability, precision and accuracy, and technical sophistication of these and other mapping instruments vary greatly. In any given project, different instruments will be used for different jobs depending on the degree of accuracy required and the estimated budgetary limits of the project. A basic principle of every survey operation is that the surveyor should "always work from the more accurate to the less accurate methods" (Pugh 1975:xvii). Thus, a wide-ranging regional expedition may first establish a system of precisely located benchmarks with a transit. Subsequent reference points may be measured with a compass. The expense of the transit work can be minimized by renting an instrument and performing the control survey in a short period of several days. Whatever instruments are used, adherence to this principle can mean both increased accuracy and reduced cost.

The discussion of mapping would not be complete without mention of aerial photography as a mapping tool. Recent editions of the U.S. Geological Survey National Topographic Map Series have made extensive use of photographs taken from airplanes in controlled aerial surveys. With minimal ground survey controls, the maps developed from air photos are highly accurate both horizontally and vertically, are rich in detail, and may be rapidly produced. The precision and detail available cannot be matched, and cost-benefit comparisons of photogrammetric and surface mapping surveys on archaeological projects have shown that the costs are lower as well.

One of the most ambitious archaeological mapping projects ever carried out, the Teotihuacan Project (Millon 1973; Pendergast 1975), used aerial photographs to map the ruins of the largest Pre-Columbian city in North America. Constructed and occupied between about 100 B.C. and A.D. 650, Teotihuacan was the administrative and cultural center of a civilization that may have rivaled the later Aztecs, who lived in the same area and similarly established trade and political relations with nearly all of present-day Mexico and Guatemala. Immense flat-topped earthen pyramids arranged axially along a 2-kilometer-long (1.25-mile) Avenue of the Dead form the center of an urban metropolis that covered approximately 19 square kilometers (7.6 square miles) and had, at its peak, an estimated population of between 85,000 and 125,000.

Since the boundaries of Teotihuacan shifted during its 750-year history, mapping covered a larger territory than the peak population period area. In

1962 the Cia Mexicana Aerofoto made a photographic survey at an elevation of 1335 meters (4000 feet). The maps drawn from these photos were required by the archaeologist, Rene Millon, to show detail down to individual trees and shrubs at

a horizontal accuracy such that 90% of all well-defined planimetric features would be plotted to within .625 millimeter when measured on the original pencil drawings, and that no such well-defined feature would be in error by more than 1.25 millimeters. At 1:100, .625 millimeter equals 1.25 meters on the ground and 1.25 millimeters equals 2.5 meters. (Millon 1973:10.)

The photogrammetric map produced to these specifications covered an area of 55 square kilometers (22 square miles) and served as a basis for pedestrian survey of the area. One section of the mapped area is shown in Figure 3.7 along with the archaeological interpretation of the contours. Potsherds, tools of other materials, and observations of architecture and building materials collected and noted on the foot survey have enabled reconstruction of the city plan and the growth and decline of the city as a population center in the Mesoamerican Late Formative and Classic periods.

Recovery Operations

Since later chapters describe specific techniques of field work, it is unnecessary to go into great detail on the subject of recovery operations at this point. The recovery of artifacts and environmental data usually are performed simultaneously, although they need not be. For example, paleoenvironmental reconstruction may be based on pollen cores obtained from lake sediments separate from archaeological zones. The techniques of recovery in such a case are quite distinct from those employed in artifact recovery, and the sampling units are obviously spatially distinct from the archaeological zones. Recognizing these differences, archaeologists conceive of environmental and artifact recovery as separate operations (see Fig. 3.1).

As discussed in an earlier section, problem formulation must decide whether or not the phenomena specified in the hypotheses have an objective existence. In the field, another aspect of implementing the terms of the hypothesis comes into focus. The degree to which the specified artifact classes can be distinguished from elements and features of the environment in which they occur must be determined. In some settings artifact classes can be easily distinguished from elements and features of the environment where they occur. Artifact recognition may be a relatively straightforward matter, as in study units that occur on or in alluvial deposits composed of sediments no coarser than sand. In other settings, artifact recognition may

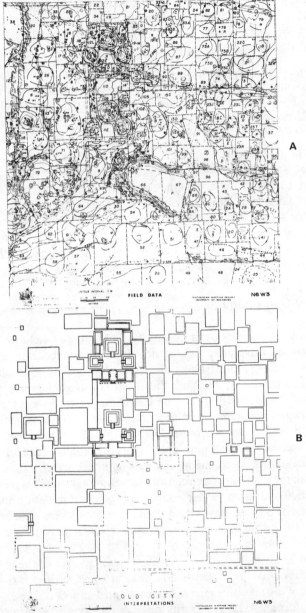

Figure 3.7. Details of the archaeological map of Teotihuacan, Mexico. (A) Field data for a section of the site. (B) Interpretation of the field data showing locations of structures and pyramids. (From Millon 1973)

be complicated by the fact that the natural deposits are composed of elements, or clusters of elements, occurring at the same scale as the archaeological phenomena of interest, or the fact that geological processes or animal activity may modify the deposit (or elements of it) in ways similar or identical to cultural processes. For instance, flints and cherts occur naturally in abundance in many parts of the world and may be fractured by percussion through frost cracking or erosional processes. In such areas, an investigator must grapple with the problem of distinguishing natural from artificial materials in designing and executing a research design calling for recovery of by-products of toolmaking. These by-products consist of discarded flakes and chips of stone which are collectively referred to as *debitage*.

The recovery of information on housing and other structures in the archaeological deposits of people whose constructions were framed with poles set in the ground presents another problem of this sort. Small rodents commonly inhabit such settlements in the postdepositional phase and their burrows are often the same size and have the same coloration as the post mold traces of former man-made structures. Vertical cross-sectioning of circular stains often can resolve the problem, but in many instances this procedure is inconclusive or uneconomical. Faced with just this problem on a massive scale at the Utz Site in Missouri, Van der Merwe and Stein (1972) were forced to develop a soil-chemistry definition of post mold to make the distinction accurately and quickly in the field. While these examples may represent extreme cases, in all archaeological field research it is necessary to construct an explicit, situational definition of artifact tailored not only to the requirements of the problem but to the conditions of the study area as well. Because this tailoring operation combines knowledge of natural and artificial characteristics of the study area, it is shown in the model (Fig. 3.1) as occurring between "environmental recovery" and "artifact recovery."

The nature of a given problem determines the approach to environmental and artifact recovery in any given study. It is not possible to give a cookbook formula for this aspect of applying research design. It may be useful, however, to summarize a model devised by Redman (1973) as a general guide to the recovery of regional settlement patterns. This model formalizes an approach pioneered by Binford (1964) and elaborated by Struever (1968).

The Redman model, called a *regional multistage field research design*, consists of four basic methods arranged in a series of stages. As shown in Figure 3.8, the model encourages feedback between stages. In terms of the model, an initial general reconnaissance is followed by an intensive survey, controlled surface collection, and excavation, in that order. Beginning with

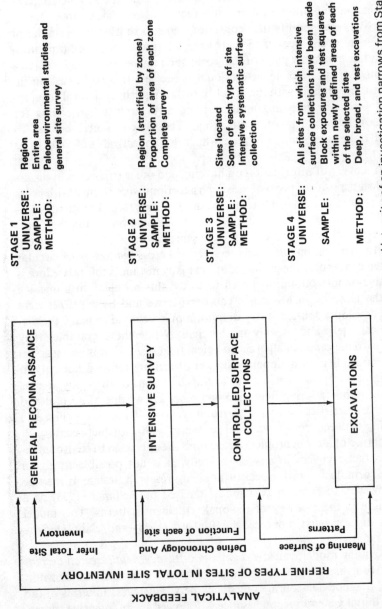

STAGE 1
UNIVERSE: Region
Entire area
SAMPLE:
METHOD: Paleoenvironmental studies and
general site survey

STAGE 2
UNIVERSE: Region (stratified by zones)
SAMPLE: Proportion of area of each zone
METHOD: Complete survey

STAGE 3
UNIVERSE: Sites located
SAMPLE: Some of each type of site
METHOD: Intensive, systematic surface
collection

STAGE 4
UNIVERSE: All sites from which intensive
surface collections have been made
SAMPLE: Block exposures and test squares
within newly defined areas of each
of the selected sites
METHOD: Deep, broad, and test excavations

GENERAL RECONNAISSANCE

INTENSIVE SURVEY

CONTROLLED SURFACE
COLLECTIONS

EXCAVATIONS

Inventory
Infer Total Site

Function of each site
Define Chronology And

Patterns
Meaning of Surface

REFINE TYPES OF SITES IN TOTAL SITE INVENTORY

ANALYTICAL FEEDBACK

Figure 3.8. A regional multistage field research design. The scope and intensity of an investigation narrows from Stage 1 to Stage 4. Analysis performed concurrently with the field research can aid in the evaluation and refinement of the recovery strategy as work proceeds. (Adapted from Redman 1973 by permission of The Society for American Archaeology from *American Antiquity* 38:61-79.)

a large area, research narrows progressively in scale, culminating with the excavation of a small, carefully selected sample of sites. Except in the first stage, probability sampling guides the selection choices.

Stage 1 is a general reconnaissance of the region and involves observation of the natural environment, site location, and other features of the archaeological material in the region. It is like the similarly named military practice of scouting an area in a circumspect but partial way before launching a massive and thorough battle attack. Familiarity with the terrain is achieved, a preliminary picture of the nature and complexity of the archaeological record is gained, and data for an ecological structuring of the environment necessary for Stage 2 are collected. The probability sampling design is "tied in" to the landscape and adjusted or modified as field conditions, detailed mapping, and environmental study require.

In Stage 2 the researcher conducts an intensive surface survey of selected portions of the region. All archaeological materials in the sampling units are located and related to environmental features. Samples are taken of all artifact clusters and features (such as architectural remains). The information from this stage is analyzed to determine settlement type, chronology, and other characteristics that will allow preliminary study of the prehistoric use of the region.

Stage 3 consists of an intensification of the controlled surface collection begun in Stage 2. Whereas in Stage 2, data on site size, extent of habitation, activities performed, and time of occupation are sought, the Stage 3 operations require detailed information on functional differentiation within the site boundaries and chronological development of the settlements. This means more comprehensive coverage and larger samples. Thus, Stage 3 narrows the scope of the project while intensifying the examination of specific locations (sites). Only select examples of the Stage 2 settlement types and time periods are investigated in this stage.

Stage 4 is the actual excavation stage. The scope of the project is further narrowed as representative sites are chosen from the groups of Stage 3 sites. These sites are then excavated to obtain information on subsurface features and on stratigraphic relations between different layers (if the site is stratified). According to this model, excavation serves the function of providing structural and ecological information unavailable at the surface. For example, intensive surface collection may indicate that a group of sites share agricultural tools and a circular community layout. Excavation of the site may show that the circular pattern on the surface is a reflection of a circular, stockaded town in which houses were arranged around an open central area barren of artifacts. Study of faunal and floral remains from the houses and the evidence of tools from dump areas may confirm that these stockaded towns were inhabited by agriculturalists. The general pattern postulated from earlier stages is thus verified, refined, and given substance in the excavation stage.

Actual Versus Expected Recovery

By synthesizing the elements of research design discussed in this chapter, one can frame a general picture of the kind of information needed for solution of the problem. This constitutes the "expected recovery" of the design. Rarely is this expectation fulfilled, and actual recovery must be compared with expected recovery to determine whether the problem can be solved. Any difference between expected and actual recovery is termed *bias*. While bias is not considered in detail in this chapter, its effects on artifact recovery are noted. Many factors influence recovery. For example, artifacts can be too deeply buried to be discovered, except by accident. Or some crew members may be vastly more skilled than others, and some lazier, with the result that the collections reflect patterns of skill and motivation in the crew instead of patterns of prehistoric activity. And some kinds of artifacts may blend into the soil while others stand out to become disproportionately represented in the sample. Factors such as these must be considered before recovered material can be regarded as data. If the biases are deemed unacceptable, the project may have to be redone, as shown by the feedback loop in the diagram (Fig. 3.1). Fortunately, most biases are technical in nature and can be corrected in a second season of work.

Collections that have passed the bias test must be evaluated even further before they can be accepted as data for solution of the problem. One of the most common problems of archaeological field work is that not enough material is recovered. This may require that the investigation enter a second season. Another common problem is inadequate sampling design. In probability sampling, for example, the study area may have been partitioned in a culturally meaningless manner. Adjustment of the design may solve the problem. It is not impossible that the problem was ill-conceived. Not all problems can be solved, and in spite of serious, thoughtful planning, the field work may simply show that data for the problem do not exist. In such a case, it may be wise, Figure 3.1 indicates, to abandon the research.

Summary

Archaeological data recovery is a complex process that requires extensive background preparation before the actual business of field work begins. Preparation here does not merely mean equipment assembly, transportation arrangements, land access permissions, and other logistic matters. It means logical consideration of the reason for doing the research and the manner in which the research must be carried out to be successful. Logistic considerations may enter into decisions that are made at this strategic level, but they are not addressed in detail.

In essence, the topics discussed in this chapter are elements of research design, although this term embraces a great deal more than has been included here. Problem formulation, hypothesis construction, sampling design, and the other topics form the early stages of research design. A complete design is a blueprint that outlines the research from field recovery and analysis to hypothesis testing and on to problem solution. To appreciate the importance of the pre-data-recovery elements of the design, it is instructive to consider the purpose of a research design as a whole. "The function of a research design is to organize the procedures of study so that error is minimized, effort is economized, and relevant evidence is gathered efficiently" (Lastrucci 1967:105). In other words, scientific research must be done in an orderly, controlled, economical fashion to be successful. Sound construction of research design is the way to ensure success.

Chapter 4

Common Elements of Archaeological Field Techniques

If one could visit one hundred archaeological projects around the world, one would be struck initially by the great diversity among them. Environment, geological characteristics, kinds and preservation of artifacts, type of site, numbers and skill of workers, nationality and background of the director and staff—these and myriad other factors affect the process and product of archaeology. In spite of the great differences, however, standard guidelines are followed by field workers everywhere. A universal set of principles are employed to ensure accurate, reliable documentation of the remains being studied. These universal standards are the subject of this chapter.

At the root of all archaeological field work is the fact that the archaeological record is a nonrenewable resource. As discussed in Chapter 2, investigation itself destroys the subtle relationships between items, and between items and their environment. Only when field work centers on surface exposures and nothing is removed is this not true. A general guideline in archaeology, therefore, is that the records of an investigation must be so detailed and precise that the deposit can be reconstructed from them.

On a more specific level, at least four features are common to archaeological investigations. They are stated briefly here and will be elaborated later in the chapter.

1. Archaeological investigations are conducted within clearly defined units to provide a control framework for artifact location, recording, and collecting. The squares of a graph-paper-like grid are the most common form of adherence to this principle.

2. Natural units have precedence over arbitrary units. The boundaries of a grid square are artificial and arbitrary. They are determined by the archaeologist as a means of controlling an investigation and have no meaning in reference to the behavior fossilized in the archaeological

record. Great care must be taken, therefore, in the identification of units of natural association.

3. The locations of artifacts are recorded as precisely as possible. For manufactured tools and ornaments, and for the items composing a feature, exact locations are required in most situations. Industrial and food waste, such as chipped stone flakes and bone fragments, may be recorded with less precision. The squares of a grid system, or segments of a square, often give sufficient locational control for such material.

4. The matrix in which artifacts are embedded is recorded. Artifact locations alone do not form an adequate archaeological record. It is imperative that the physical context of the finds be recorded as well, to evaluate the quality of data recovery and the extent of decay, to determine the stratigraphic relationships of artifacts, and to enable reconstruction of the prevailing natural environment.

Framework of Investigation

The most conspicuous feature of an excavation is the orderliness of the layout. Few if any other activities that involve digging into the ground pay as much attention to control of the size, shape, and relative placement of holes as does archaeology. House and road construction trenches approximate this orderliness in that precision instruments are used to guide workers. Stakes are carefully positioned to mark building corners and points on rights-of-way. The precision is applied only to the margins of the house or highway, however, and the holes where the house or the highway will be located are dug with great abandon. Similarly, the holes of ditch-digging for a pipeline would hardly be confused with archaeological trenches because once again placement of the pipe is the important objective, not the actual digging of the hole. Precisely oriented and clearly defined units are hallmarks that make archaeological excavations, and other investigations, recognizable even from great distances.

The term applied to the uniform stake layouts in archaeology is *grid system*. Investigations which are not organized in reference to a grid system are usually the work of vandals or of lay archaeologists ignorant of the basic field work principles. Nonprofessional, ungridded excavations resemble prairie dog towns of the western states (Fig. 4.1). Mounds of dirt alternating with depressions of varying sizes and shapes are strewn randomly over a field. Order is totally lacking in the work and presumably in the records as well.

A

B

Figure 4.1. Destructive and scientific archaeological excavation. (A) Digging of the sort shown here ignores established principles of observation, recording, and recovery, and results in the destruction of the archaeological record. (Reproduced by permission of The Arkansas Archaeological Society.) (B) Adherence to established principles produces a documented record of artifact distributions (Reproduced by permission of *Archaeology* 24:300-306, 1971.)

One very important function of the grid system in archaeology is to permit precise placement of sampling units (pits and trenches). Grid systems have at least three other functions. First, the grid permits accurate measurement of artifact locations. For example, before an ornamental item is removed from a burial, the artifact must be drawn on a scale map of the skeleton to preserve a record of its location relative to other artifacts and to the bones of the skeleton. Secondly, grids are useful in planning. Archaeologically, the columns and rows of a grid system allow orderly expansion of an excavation. Additionally, most field workers use a standard-sized grid unit and know the time and labor required to examine one unit to a given depth. Thus, a director can plan appropriately.

The third reason to use grid systems is to facilitate recording the progress of work. In excavation, pits are frequently filled with the dirt of a subsequent pit. The job of filling in the excavation at the end of the project is reduced in this way, but the progress of work is obscured. Scale maps of the excavated grid units give a picture of the parts of the site that have been dug. On a larger scale, archaeological survey of a region can be greatly aided by working within grid units. As one roams widely over the land, it is easy to lose track of the ground one has covered. Carrying a gridded map of the region, a field worker can systematically check off grid units as they are traversed on the ground. In short, grid systems tell you where you are, where you have been, and where you are going.

One decision to be made when deciding upon a grid system concerns the size of the grid squares. There is no magic number dictating a requisite size of archaeological squares. The choice depends in the first place on the space that allows a worker sufficient room for maneuverability. The size of the area under investigation and the nature of the archaeological remains also are important considerations. When the English measurement system was used, 5-foot or 10-foot squares were common. With the introduction of the metric system, one- and 2-meter squares have become popular.

Another factor in designing a grid concerns how grid units are labeled. One of the simplest systems is to give the grid squares numerical or alphabetical designations (Fig. 4.2A). Another possibility is to label the rows and columns of the system, giving one axis numerical designations and the other one alphabetical designations. A given square is referred to by the appropriate number and letter of the intersecting axes (Fig. 4.2B). A third alternative is to label the intersecting lines that form the grid. In this system the lines rather than the spaces are designated, resulting in a label for unit corners rather than the units themselves. By convention, grids are oriented to the cardinal directions and squares are labeled starting from the southwest corner (Fig. 4.2C). Which system is used in any given study is largely a matter of preference and convenience.

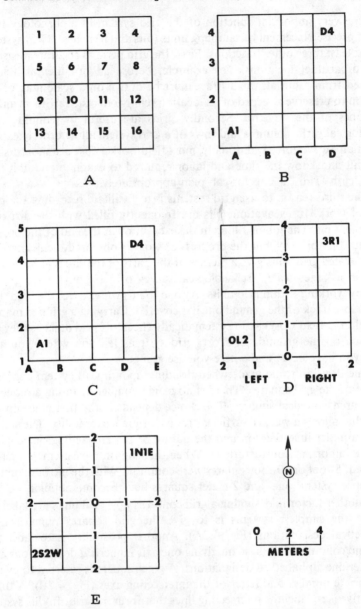

Figure 4.2. Five systems of grid unit designation.

In practice, there are many variations of these basic systems. One traditional system (Cole and Deuel 1937) combines numerical designation for the intervals on both axes and a left and right designation for one of the axes, with the remaining axis serving as base line. A diagram of this system is shown in Figure 4.2D. Using the southwest corners to designate a square, the square in the upper right of the figure is 4R1 and the one in the lower left is 0L2. This system works best when the extent of remains is well known so that the "0" point, or *datum,* can be located outside the area of investigation. A grid of this type can be greatly expanded to the left or right of base line, but expansion in the direction opposite the intersecting axis requires addition of a plus and minus symbol to intervals on this axis. This problem can be skirted if the system is embedded in a more comprehensive grid, as was done at the Angel Site, a fifteenth-century A.D. stockaded town in southern Indiana, shown in Figure 4.3.

A system that permits unlimited expansion in all directions by use of numerical and directional designations for each grid intersection or interval is in wide use. In Figure 4.2E, points are numbered and the axes are labeled in reference to the cardinal directions. On the axes then, we have 1 North, 2 North, 1 East, 2 East and so forth. Moving away from datum, the upper left point in the grid is 2 North, 2 West. Using southwest corners to label squares, the upper left square is 2 North 2 West and the lower right is 2 South 1 East. This system is useful because of its flexibility, but care must be exercised to orient it as closely as possible to true north. An example of this type of system as used in the investigation of the Classic Period Mexican city of Teotihuacan is shown in Figure 4.4.

It should be emphasized that grids are important in controlling large-scale regional investigations as well as individual site studies. An example of a regional grid can be found in the work of Thomas (1974:37-43) in the Reese River Valley, Nevada (Fig. 4.5). Thomas's research focused upon prehistoric occupation of the various ecological zones of a semiarid valley in Nevada, and particularly in obtaining archaeological data for comparison with Shoshone Indian lifeways. The Shoshone and their ancestors were nomadic peoples who lived by hunting and gathering wild foods and who moved their settlements according to the dictates of seasonal variation in resource availability. Study of recent and prehistoric Shoshone lifeways, therefore, requires a regional research area, and Thomas chose a portion of the Reese River Valley in central Nevada as his sampling universe or study area. In an area 18 kilometers (11 miles) wide and 26 kilometers (16 miles) long, he sent out teams to inspect 140 survey tracts, each 500 meters square, for traces of human utilization. The selected squares constituted a 10 percent sample of squares in a grid system that had been superimposed on

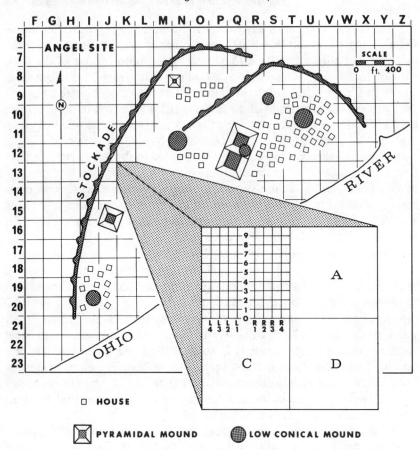

Figure 4.3. Site map of the Angel Site, Indiana. Each unit in the master 200-foot-interval grid system is divided into four 100-foot units which are in turn divided into 10-foot squares. As shown, the grid squares at each scale are designated by different systems. (Adapted from *Angel Site*, by Glenn A. Black, Figures 8, 9, 14, and 546. Indianapolis: Indiana Historical Society. 1967.)

maps and aerial photographs of the region. The study produced evidence that a way of life similar to that of the historic period Shoshone bands characterized Native American societies of the area as long ago as 2500 B.C.

The grid system establishes horizontal control, and for surface investigations this is all that is needed. In excavation, however, care is taken to control the vertical dimension. The basic concept of vertical control is the datum plane. This is an arbitrary point of reference that may be described

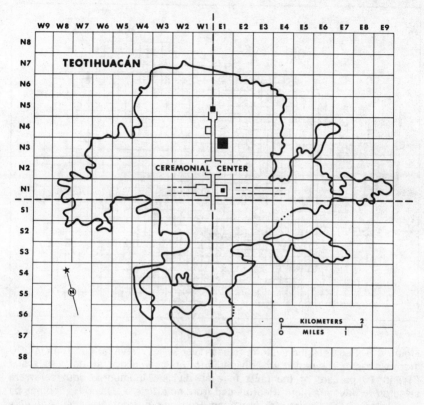

Figure 4.4. Site map of Teotihuacan, Mexico, showing the system of grid control. The bold line indicates the maximum boundary of the site. (From Millon 1973)

as an imaginary level that extends through the site at some convenient elevation. The concept of mean sea level is an example of a datum plane on a global scale which standardizes measurements of the earth's surface.

In recording observations, items located above the datum plane are given "plus" notations and items below it are marked as "minus." The plane can be designated as "zero" with all measurements given meaning with reference solely to the grid. Alternatively the elevation of the plane above or below sea level can be determined by surveying methods and measurements within the grid recorded in reference to the global system. The latter approach is important where artifact locations within a number of sites are being related to topographic features such as river terraces. Otherwise, intrasite recording is most conveniently done with a local point of reference.

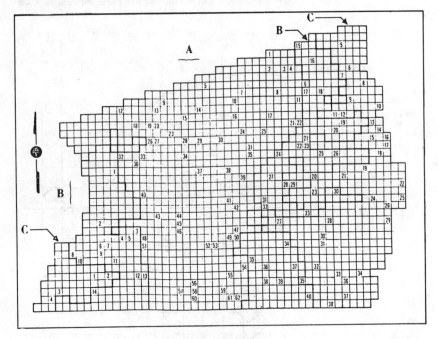

Figure 4.5. Regional grid system, Reese River Valley, Nevada. Each unit is 500 meters square. The region was divided into three sampling "strata" (A, B, and C) and 10 percent of the units in each division (numbered squares) were selected for investigation. (Reproduced from an article by David H. Thomas by permission of The Society for American Archaeology from *American Antiquity* 38:169, 1973.)

With the datum plane established, vertical control is ensured through the use of levels. When digging, archaeologists find it helpful to clear off a working floor at the bottom of a pit or trench to inspect the ground for post molds, fire basins, and other features. This is best done by digging a uniform interval, such as 6 inches or 20 centimeters. As with grid squares, the interval selected depends on specific dimensions of the deposit, such as total depth and number of strata. Each interval is referred to as a level and is labeled either sequentially from datum plane (level 1, level 2, etc.) or with the depth figures (0 to −10 level, −10 to −20 level, etc.). In essence, a system of levels creates a vertical grid and combined with the horizontal grid it can give an extra measure of control to the work.

Natural Units

Grid systems have an obvious benefit in exercising control over the work. However, the grid should not become so important in a field worker's mind that it obscures the natural physical structure of the surface or subsurface remains. An ever-present danger in field work is that artifact locations will be recorded in the grid system without additional reference to the physical unit containing the items. An important principle of archaeological field method, therefore, is that natural units have precedence over arbitrary units.

A few words on the meaning of natural unit are in order before we look at the consequences of violating the principle and at the interaction of grid and natural units. The term "natural" conveys the idea of geological, biological, or any other feature that results from physical rather than human cultural and social processes. Most archaeologists, however, expand the meaning of natural to mean any unit of matter whose boundaries are abrupt changes in composition, color, or other measurable attributes. This definition includes units that are both physically and culturally formed and does not presume which of various processes are specifically involved.

The earthen burial mounds characteristic of American Indian cultures of the eastern United States between 1000 B.C. and A.D. 900 provide good examples of various kinds of natural units that have been culturally formed (Fig. 4.6). In the early periods of the mound burial mortuary practice, people of the Adena cultural tradition (Dragoo 1963) followed a standardized procedure of disposal of the dead which resulted in hills of dirt reaching as high as 21.5 meters (70 feet) containing numerous burials at various levels. The initial event in the growth of these mounds is thought by some archaeologists to have been the conversion of a domestic structure to a charnel house upon the death of the resident, who may have been an important person in the community. Shallow pits about 2 feet deep were often dug in the floor of the structure and the walls lined with logs. Subsequent to burial, the log tomb was covered with branches and finally with a layer of dirt. Dish-shaped basins were often prepared instead of deeper graves. Upon accumulation of a number of burials on or below the floor, the structure was burned to the ground and a layer of dirt or gravel laid over the ashes. The mounds usually were given a conical shape. At later dates, the surface of the mound often served for additional burials. A mound used in this way grew in height over the years. In contrast to our cemeteries, which grow laterally over time, Adena cemeteries grew vertically.

A number of different natural units are present in Adena burial mounds. Most obvious are the graves, particularly the log tomb variety

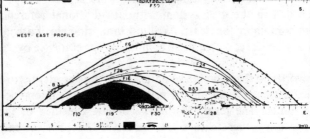

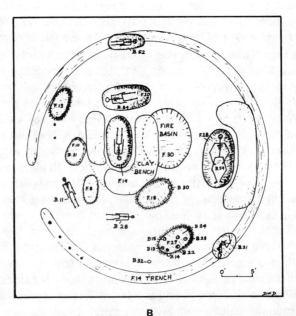

Figure 4.6. Stratigraphic profile and ground plan of the Cresap Mound, West Virginia. The mound grew in height as burials were added and covered with layers of sediment (A). The plan (B) shows the major features and burials found on or below the clay floor of the mound. (Reproduced from Dragoo 1963 by permission of The Carnegie Museum of Natural History.)

which usually have clearly defined boundaries. The different layers of dirt piled over graves also constitute natural units and usually appear archaeologically as distinct strata. A more subtle natural unit is the charnel house, evidence of which may be present in the form of circular stains where the posts forming the walls once penetrated ground surface and rotted after burning and burial. The space within the house would be an important natural unit since it can be assumed that artifacts within the walls were associated with the domestic functions performed before change in its function, and with ceremonial ritual after its conversion to a charnel house. Fire basins related to food preparation, ritual activity, or cremation may also be present at various levels of the mound; each constitutes a distinct natural unit. The layers of dirt in these mounds were constructed of clay dug from nearby locations and carried to the burial site in flat baskets or similar containers. The individual basket loads are often visible in excavation pit walls and each "load" constitutes a natural unit, although their small size makes it impractical to remove them one by one in excavation.

In a subsurface context, therefore, any recognizably distinct segment of dirt is considered a natural unit. In the Adena mound example, all units were humanly formed, but such is not always the case. For example, the remains of a settlement located at the edge of an annually flooding river would contain natural units as a result of both cultural and physical processes. Because of flooding, the site would show multiple layers of flood silt and sand. The human occupants may have lived in pole and thatch houses which would, along with the post molds, constitute natural units. Fires may have been laid in rock-lined basins; food may have been stored in clay-lined pits; the remains are considered natural units.

Pueblo ruins in the American Southwest contain the remains of clay and stone wall structures consisting of multiple, conjoined rooms (McGregor 1965). These famous, apartmentlike communities crumble upon abandonment and are covered with drifting and windborne sand and silt. Excavation typically reveals layers representing rebuilding phases, rooms for various purposes, religious structures dug partially or completely below surface, and multiple layering in rooms that represents periodic replastering of floors. In rooms and courtyards, fire basins are found, as are post molds from benches, verandas, cooking shelters, and other special structures. All of these constitute natural units and potentially contain meaningful associations of artifacts that permit reconstruction of a site's history and the activities performed in the various rooms and sections of the village.

The reason it is important to specify that natural units take precedence over grid units is that artifacts from adjacent natural units may become mixed together if the principle is not observed. In the excavation of a pueblo ruin, for example, the wall foundations may not be visible on the surface, and artifact collection and recording initially would use the grid units to maintain a record of horizontal separation of excavated finds. As the walls of the pueblo rooms emerge, it is highly unlikely that the floorplan of the structure will correspond to the cells of the grid system. Grid units will overlap adjacent rooms or possibly even include two or more rooms. To continue collection of broken pottery fragments, stone tools, and other debris in terms of the grid units would mix artifacts from different rooms and make study of chronological and functional differences between rooms impossible.

Mixing on a horizontal basis where standing walls are encountered, as in the pueblo example, is probably rare. Usually the natural units are quite obvious both as physical phenomena and as important units of analysis. Vertical strata and pits, however, present real difficulties and cases of jumbled layers are abundant in the literature. Mixing usually results from an inability to detect strata composed of similar sediments. Frequently, however, the problem arises because the convenience of the grid levels for bagging artifacts overshadows close attention to changes in soil texture, color, and composition which, though faint, may be defined clearly enough to give a uniform basis for collection.

Quite a controversy has developed in the literature over the use of arbitrary levels in vertical excavation (Hester, Heizer, and Graham 1975:79-84). Many excavators regard evenly measured, vertical levels as unnecessary and dangerous. Strata are proclaimed the only legitimate vertical guide to excavation. It might be argued, for instance, that in a site with a shell bottom layer one meter (3 feet) thick, an organic-rich black middle layer 5 meters (1.5 feet) thick, and a pottery-laden reddish top layer 0.3 meter (one foot) thick, excavation in 10-centimeter (4-inch) arbitrary levels would unnecessarily complicate the record, retard progress, and without question obscure the boundaries between strata. Defenders of arbitrary units might reply that strata such as these rarely accumulate as a single event and that a record of temporal change is present within each of the distinct strata, with earlier artifacts at the bottom and later ones at the top. Important data on cultural change are lost, therefore, if the strata are excavated as units and artifacts bagged indiscriminately from each. Arbitrary units that segregate artifacts from top, bottom, and intermediate portions surmount the problem. Furthermore, arbitrary levels do not themselves produce mixing; human abuse of the system creates the problem. Skillful digging and the separation of artifacts from several strata that are crosscut by a single level provides the required stratigraphic record.

In concluding this section, it may be pointed out that the arbitrary units of a grid system have an important role in maintaining order both in excavation and in surface work. They must not be confused with the natural units whose discovery and documentation are the major objective of field work. On the other hand, they need not be discarded once natural units are found. The most successful piece of archaeological work will be the one which recognizes the proper function of the two kinds of units and uses them in conjunction to obtain a full and controlled record.

Locational Recording

Let us turn to some concepts and practical matters related to recording locations. First of all, archaeological field records, reports, and popular accounts contain frequent reference to the *provenience* of a find. Provenience is a precise term for "location" and is preferred because of the multiple, differing meanings of the more common term location. Secondly, it is useful to distinguish *planimetric* from three-dimensional recording systems. Planimetric systems are two-dimensional and do not include measurements of elevation and depression. The planimetric, or horizontal, data combined with vertical measurements give a three-dimensional provenience record.

The principles of planimetric recording as expounded in surveying and mapping texts are lengthy and involved. For our purposes discussion may be restricted to two of the most common systems: *triangulation* and *coordinate recording*. Triangulation is the measurement of an unknown point in reference to two known points the distance between which is recorded. Each known point is called a datum. On a small scale, imagine an intact pottery vessel unearthed in the center portion of a 2-meter-square grid unit of an excavation (Fig. 4.7A). Two of the stakes marking the square's corners can serve as datums. The square is designated 6 North 0 East after the southwest corner stake, and the pot measures 1.5 meters from the northwest stake and one meter from the southwest stake (6 North 0 East). This information is recorded in a notebook along with a number given to the pot for cataloging purposes. At the time of recording, or later during laboratory analysis, a map may be drawn showing the provenience of the pot and other items and features from the square and adjacent squares.

Coordinate recording, in which grid coordinates of an item are determined, is another way of measuring planimetric provenience. The axes, or base lines, of the grid are the basic points of reference, and measurements are made perpendicular to each axis to pinpoint a location. Internally, with a grid that is physically segmented into squares, as is the case with most archaeological grids, the boundaries of a square can serve as reference lines. Returning to our imaginary pot (Fig. 4.7B), it is 0.75 meter from the south wall of square 6 North 0 East and 0.75 meter from the west wall. Apart

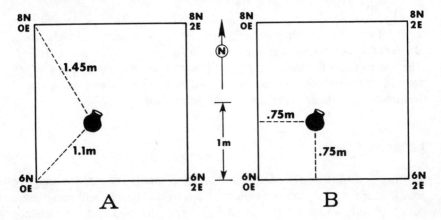

Figure 4.7. Triangulation (A) and coordinate (B) recording of an item in an excavation square.

from the act of measurement, this data is recorded in the same way as triangulation data.

Without the *vertical* dimension in an excavation, the record of an item's provenience is incomplete. Measurement of the vertical distance of the item above or below the principal grid datum or a secondary datum at some other position in the grid is needed. One common method (Fig. 4.8) of obtaining this information is to erect a telescopic level over the datum and to determine the distance of the telescope above the item in question as sighted on a graduated rod held vertically on or next to the item. The distance of the telescope above the datum is then subtracted from the reading on the rod to obtain the measurement of the item above or below the datum.

Let us now consider another type of location, the *unit location*. In contrast to exact location, in which the three-dimensional coordinates of an item are determined, the unit location consists of the space within which the item or a group of items are located. Recording in a notebook that our imaginary pot was found in level 3 of square 6 North 0 East gives a general idea of its position in the grid system, but does not pinpoint its location. For manufactured tools, like our pot, a unit location is insufficient, but if thousands of sherds are encountered, unit location is appropriate and useful. Debris such as potsherds, the flakes from stone chipping, and broken bones in a garbage deposit may be too numerous to be recorded exactly. However, collected as a group and stored in a bag marked with the square and level, such debris can be very useful in reconstructing prehistoric life, even without exact location for each.

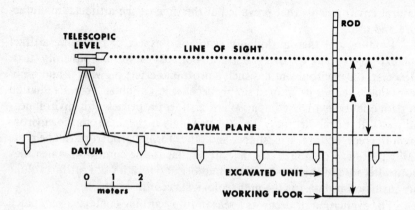

Figure 4.8. Recording vertical measurements in archaeological excavation. The depth of the working floor of the excavation unit below the datum plane is determined by subtracting the instrument height (B) from the measurement of the distance between the working floor and the instrument line of sight (A).

Context

Although much of the discussion thus far has centered on controlling and measuring artifact locations, it should not be forgotten that locational information is incomplete without knowledge of the context of an array of finds. Context means the surroundings, or environment, of the finds. In the case of an excavated stone axe or bone needle, a description of the soil encasing the objects is necessary. A stray projectile point found on the surface must be related to the vegetation, soils, and slope of the place it was found. Information on the geological and biotic surroundings of a site is an important part of the archaeological record. At an even larger scale, it is often necessary to record the general physiographic area where a given find occurs. In other words, locational data about artifacts must be supplemented by information on their specific and general environment.

Context is important for four basic reasons. First, context is necessary to evaluate the quality of data recovery. Differences in soil color and texture, for example, affect a field worker's ability to perceive archaeological material. Next, it permits evaluation of the extent of decay in altering the physical and chemical makeup of materials. This is particularly important in subsurface deposits. In the third place, contextual data are required to determine the stratigraphic relationships of artifacts. Are objects found within a few centimeters of one another contemporaneous, or are some of them at the bottom of a pit dug from a higher level at a later date? Finally, records and examples of artifact context can be used to reconstruct the natural environments that prevailed at the time of the artifacts' manufacture and use.

Pointing out the data quality evaluation aspect of recording artifact context may seem to overreach the bounds of an introductory text. However, the environment has such a profound effect on what is and is not seen, that it cannot be ignored simply because it it a subtle topic. Evaluation of data quality involves comparison of artifact properties with environmental characteristics. Artifacts that are strikingly different from the environment in color, texture, size, shape, and other formal properties will be more easily perceived than artifacts that are similar to the context in which they occur. Because of this, notes on the number and locations of artifacts alone are insufficient data for the archaeological record.

The evaluation of decay as a reason for recording context is very much like evaluation of perception bias. Quite obviously, the archaeological record is strongly affected by the preservative properties of the environment. Completely dry environments usually preserve organic and inorganic materials to a higher degree than do environments that receive moisture, even if only an inch or two annually. However, perpetually waterlogged environments are noted for their excellent preservation of inorganic remains. Bogs in many parts of the world have yielded human and animal remains with skin, hair, and bone intact. The bones, however, lack the calcium which gave them rigidity during life and can literally be tied in knots.

Although this is not the place to discuss the subject of decay in detail, it is crucial to point out that preservative qualities of soil can differ over very short distances, even several centimeters. No archaeological record is complete without the measurement or sampling of such decay factors as moisture content, acidity, and temperature.

As an example of the problems that may arise from failure to record such information, consider a study investigating the degree to which hunting is a part of the food-getting economy. Bones are an important source of information, but they are also fragile materials that frequently perish in the soil. If the study is set in an area that has a wide variety of acid and basic soils with archaeological sites on both soil types, excavation will produce a highly distorted picture of hunting practices. All early period sites may be on acid soils which preserve little if any bone, while late period sites may be on bone-preserving alkaline soils. To conclude that hunting was unimportant in the early period clearly would be in error, but without information on soil context, such an interpretation may well be made and go unchallenged.

The third reason for recording context involves stratigraphy, the interpretation of site strata. The nature of stratification was discussed in

Chapter 2, so we may move directly to an example of the value of detailed stratigraphic records for unraveling the past. The example comes from excavations by Francois Bordes at Combe-Grenal, southwestern France (Bordes 1972). The site is a rock shelter in limestone cliffs and was occupied between 50,000 and 35,000 years ago by peoples of the Mousterian cultural tradition. Excavation of this important Middle Paleolithic site revealed 64 strata and a complex sequence of different kinds and styles of Mousterial tools.

Analyzing the results of one season's work, Bordes found an association of tool types not encountered before in Mousterian sites. Stratum J included a unique proportion of scraping and shredding tools that led Bordes to suspect inaccurate observation of stratification in the original work (Fig. 4.9). In later seasons, unexcavated portions of the rock shelter containing layer J were examined closely for an answer to the problem. It was found that the surface of layer J had been exposed to weathering for some time in the past and that water draining across the cave surface had eroded shallow gullies in various places. Tools of later occupants of the shelter settled into the gullies and during excavation were recorded as being from layer J rather than from the overlying layer I. The subtle differences between the soil of layer J and of the layer I gullies had not been perceived initially and a mixing of deposits occurred. Had Bordes not been skeptical of the analysis and persistent in clarifying the issue, a new archaeological culture might have been postulated which in reality was the result of incomplete records of stratigraphic context rather than the debris of a cohesive, distinctive human group.

The final reason for making detailed records of context is that of providing data from which reconstructions of past environments can be made. For most studies in prehistory, it is not enough to know about the culture of the past human communities. Although not necessarily determined by environment, culture is strongly affected by it, and many aspects of daily life and cultural change can be understood only in the context of the contemporary natural world. The kinds of plant pollen, the sizes, shapes, and surface conditions of sediment particles, the zonal characteristics of the soil—these and many other features of the archaeological context are keys to prehistoric climate, vegetation, season, and local terrain (Butzer 1971).

So much for the reasons for recording contextual information. How does one go about making the records? The guidelines for recording context are, in fact, the same as for artifacts, except that because the context is always more massive than the artifact component of a deposit, collection of samples requires more selective procedures. The grids used to control investigation and record artifact locations can be used for environmental data,

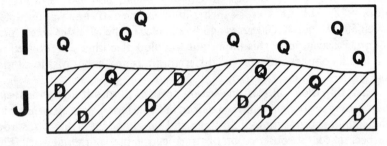

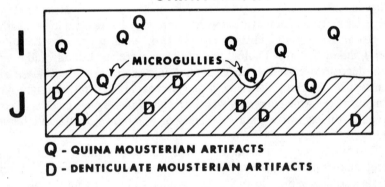

Figure 4.9. Apparent and actual stratigraphy in a portion of the Combe-Grenal Rockshelter, France. Layer J was initially thought to contain artifacts characteristic of two varieties (Quina and Denticulate) of Mousterian (Middle Paleolithic) assemblages. Subsequent analysis of the stratification disclosed microgullies in the eroded surface of Layer J. The Quina artifacts were in these gullies and thus associated with Layer I and not with Layer J. (Adapted from Bordes 1972.)

and independent systems can be established where data outside an artifact zone is sought. Locations of recorded and collected environmental data are noted as precisely as for artifacts. In short, the contextual data must be controlled in exactly the same manner as the artifact data.

Summary

Archaeological investigations around the world, although quite different in many respects, have several characteristics in common. They are conducted within clearly defined units, usually grid squares; they give precedence to natural units over arbitrary units in the recording and collection of information; they record the locations of artifacts as exactly as possible; and they obtain information on the context of the finds. These characteristics might be said to be qualifications for professional archaeology. If they are not met, the work is less than professional, and possibly constitutes vandalism.

Grid systems are important in archaeology because they permit precise placement of sampling units, accurate measurement of artifact locations, orderly expansion of an excavation, and they are useful also in recording the progress of work. The size of the individual units in a grid system depends first of all on the amount of space needed for maneuverability and lastly on the size of the features present at the site. Many systems are available for the labeling of grid units, but fundamentally they all are variations of labeling the rows and columns or labeling the intersecting lines that form the grid. Vertical control within a grid system is achieved either by measuring from a datum plane or by establishing a vertical grid of levels.

In all archaeological field work, whether on the surface or below surface, it must be recognized that the objective is to determine the relationship of artifacts to the units of natural association. Such units include geological strata, house rooms, pits, burials, and any other unit of matter whose boundaries display abrupt changes in physical characteristics. The units of a grid are used for locational control only when they crosscut natural units; the latter must be given preference in recording and collecting. The consequence of violating this rule is that units of cultural meaning will be mixed and interpretation imperfect.

Two degrees of precision in locational recording are recognized in archaeology. One is exact location in which the precise coordinates of a find are noted. This can be achieved by the common methods of triangulation or coordinate recording. A lesser degree of precision is obtained in unit location. In this case, artifacts are recorded in reference to a grid unit, or a portion of it. Exact locations will be recorded in most cases for tools, ornaments, and other manufactured artifacts, and in special cases for manufacturing debris and food waste. More frequently, however, unit locations are all that are required for the latter.

It is of extreme importance that the context of archaeological finds be recorded. This information is necessary in order to evaluate the quality of data recovery, to evaluate the degree of preservation and condition of the deposit, to determine stratigraphic relationships, and to obtain environmental data. In a sense this requirement is implied in the principle that natural units take precedence over arbitrary units. The natural units are the matrix in which artifacts occur. Isolating and describing natural units is the major objective of archaeological field work. Identifying contextual recording as a separate characteristic, however, serves to underscore the fact that artifact locations themselves do not constitute archaeological data.

In isolating these general characteristics from the general process of archaeological field work, the aim has been to show that archaeological field work is a predictable enterprise. Although individual archaeologists may feel this oversimplifies a complex subject, these four characteristics are fundamental to all field work. Especially for the beginner, it is useful to acknowledge but reduce the complexity so that the general outline of field strategy becomes firmly fixed and established. It will be evident that the following specific approaches to survey and excavation are founded on the principles discussed here.

Chapter 5

Archaeological Survey

Archaeological survey is an approach to data recovery that involves the examination of a specified tract of land to observe, record, and collect from the surface the visible remains of past human activity. Surveys are supplemented by subsurface probing. The size of the tract that is surveyed may differ considerably from study to study, but usually survey work is regional in scope. The comprehensiveness of any given survey may vary as well, with some surveys attempting to determine the complete range of archaeological remains in a region and others focusing upon a special class of material, such as rock art. Surface visibility varies greatly from region to region, and in arid areas a nearly complete record of archaeological variability may be exposed to view while in forested areas it may be almost totally obscured and require extensive subsurface probing. The results of a survey may in some cases be used to locate and predict the contents and structure of subsurface deposits as an aid in the selection of excavation sites. Conversely, the results of a survey may provide the data necessary for the direct test of research hypotheses, without excavation (Judge 1973).

In this chapter, consideration is given first to some of the common concerns of survey work and then to the major factors which influence the probability of artifact discovery. Subsequently, two common forms of archaeological survey, distinguished on the basis of whether the site or the cultural item is the focus of survey, are described in detail. Following the discussion of site survey, several techniques of intensive examination of site surfaces are dealt with. Finally, aerial photography receives attention because this tool has come to play an increasingly prominent role in survey work. (Subsurface probing is not detailed here since most of the techniques, like shovel-testing and test-pitting, are the same as the ones described in the section on excavation testing in Chapter 6.)

Some General Concerns

One of the general concerns of archaeological survey is the adoption of a master grid for the region under investigation. Some surveys employ grids developed specifically for the project. For example, in the survey of the Reese River Valley, Nevada, described in Chapter 4, Thomas (1974) created a grid system of 500-meter-square units to control coverage of the region. Another approach is to use a conventional referential system, such as the Northwest Ordinance or the Universal Transverse Mercator systems (described below). In the former, the one-mile-square "sections" which are commonly printed on maps of the areas where the system applies, provide a convenient master grid. In the latter, 1000-meter intervals marked off on the margins of U.S. Geological Survey maps are useful for a master grid. It is not uncommon to find surveys that have used political units, such as townships, road systems, property lines, or field boundaries as a basis for gridding the survey universe. Although such units will be of unequal size and shape, in contrast to arbitrary or conventional systems, they have the advantage of being inscribed on the landscape and represented on maps and aerial photographs. The large units of the master grid may form the basis of a sampling plan (see Chapter 3), or they may provide the control system for the establishment of smaller units which are selected either on a purposive or probability basis for field examination. Detailed consideration of the questions of sample size and fraction, and of unit size and shape, can be found in an article by Plog, Plog, and Wait (1978).

The coverage of the units selected for field examination, whatever their size or shape—square units (*quadrats*) and rectangular units (*transects*) are the most common—can take one of two forms. In one form, crew members traverse the unit in an irregular fashion, grouping at various points before reaching the opposite boundary of the unit. This has been called *gang dispersal* by King (1978). The other form calls for crew members to be spaced at regular intervals which are maintained from one boundary to the other in what King refers to as *deployed dispersal*. The latter form is preferred in most cases because it permits precise determination of which parts of the unit have been viewed directly by individual crew members.

Upon encountering archaeological material, workers record observations on its characteristics in a notebook and in many cases collect samples. On surveys whose purpose is to locate sites, the notes contain information required for completion of a site survey form. This information is described in detail in a later section of this chapter. On some surveys no material is collected. Notes of the kinds of artifacts present are entered in the field notebook; tools and ornaments are drawn and photographed. More commonly, distinctive artifacts are collected and samples are taken of other kinds of exposed materials. Ceramic period sites usually are treated this way: enough sherds to estimate the age of a site are collected for laboratory analysis. The development of randomized sampling plans has cast doubt on the validity of unsystematic collection of samples, however, and most surface collecting today is done within a controlled framework. Ceramics, lithics, and other abundant materials are collected in grid units (described in Chapter 6).

Whatever the purpose of a survey, and wherever it takes place, transportation is an important tactical consideration. Survey work of regional scope requires an extensive system of developed roads for automobiles and trucks. Four-wheel drive vehicles are necessary in areas lacking roads or with poorly developed roads. In terrain that is too rough for vehicles, horses, donkeys, mules, or some other kind of pack animal may be needed. Helicopters have been used in surveys of inaccessible regions. Boats are useful for survey of river banks and lake shores. Whatever the means of mechanical or animal transportation, there is no escape from walking! Archaeologists active in survey work log thousands of miles on foot.

In comparison to the excavator, who is burdened with a large, cumbersome battery of tools, the archaeological surveyor travels light. A small backpack under most circumstances will suffice for the few required recording and collecting tools, notebooks, and maps. A notebook, pens, pencils, straightedge, drawing paper, and clipboard are the minimum supplies needed for recording. A compass is indispensible for determining map location and plotting observations. A 30- or 50-meter tape measure will be needed for setting up grids if intensive surface collection is contemplated. A mason's tuck-pointing trowel, a 3-meter tape, and a foxhole trenching shovel are all that is required if test excavation is performed on the survey. Besides collecting bags, a pocket knife, and a first-aid kit, little else is needed for survey work, although additional more sophisticated equipment may be called for or preferred on some projects.

With this general background of archaeological survey in mind, we can turn to a more specific examination of the procedure. Of particular importance is the topic of discovery probability, for many factors influence the degree of success that a surveyor has in locating artifacts.

Discovery Factors

The archaeological surveyor everywhere is constantly alert for surface exposure of artifacts and for irregularities in the environment that do not seem to be the result of natural processes or of modern land use. Cultivation exposes tools, ornaments, and other artifacts which, after a rain, are immediately obvious. On pastureland and grasslands, artifacts often can be seen in the backdirt of animal burrows or on animal paths and undeveloped roads. In forests, dirt is often exposed, along with artifacts, at the base of trees. Along active rivers, cutbanks, if not grown over with a tangle of brush, reveal artifacts and the layering of a deposit.

The archaeologist on survey also is alert for surface irregularities in topography and unusual patterns of vegetation and soil. In the eastern United States, for example, burial mounds (circular, linear, or in the shape of animals), geometric earthworks enclosing ceremonial areas, and earthen platforms are clear exceptions to the normal lay of the land. When low and extensive, they may be difficult to see from the ground; the more massive pattern often can be detected only from the air.

Where burning and large-scale waste disposal has taken place adjacent to a prehistoric settlement, the soil we see today exhibits characteristics that contrast with the normal zonal development for the area. Color differences in these altered soils often are sharp enough to enable quick identification. Subtle chemical variations may not be visible, but with intensive testing they also may reveal places of past activity. Soil differences affect plant growth, and it often happens that differences in the density, height, productivity, coloration, and other aspects of plant growth can be ascribed directly to the former presence of a settlement or encampment.

It is obvious that the location and recording of archaeological surface materials is affected by many factors, some favoring discovery and some impeding it. The conditions of discovery vary from place to place, season to season, and are increased or decreased depending on the magnitude of the material, its physical-chemical properties, distributional characteristics, accessibility, and the scope and technical sophistication of the recovery project.

Schiffer, Sullivan, and Klinger (1978) have organized the myriad of specific factors under five headings: (1) abundance, (2) clustering, (3) obtrusiveness, (4) visibility, and (5) accessibility. These concepts are defined and the most common factors associated with each one are listed in Table 5.1. Summarizing the five factors, it can be said that the greatest chance of discovery lies with material that is large, abundant, dense, nonclustered, and sharply contrastive with the biology and geology of a region where the surface/subsurface is perennially or frequently exposed. Conversely, small, rare, low-density, noncontrastive, poorly exposed, inaccessible, and clustered material has a poor chance of being discovered.

The archaeology of Mexico (Weaver 1972) illustrates the extremes of these discovery probabilities. Highland Mexico, in the Mexico City vicinity,

Table 5.1. Discovery Factors

General Factors	Definition	Specific Examples
Abundance	The frequency or prevalence of a site or artifact type in the study area	Sites and artifacts occur in highly varying quantities, from rare to abundant
Clustering	The degree to which archaeological materials are spatially aggregated	Various degrees of clustering may be found between dispersed and clustered
Obtrusiveness	The probability that particular archaeological material can be discovered by a specific technique	Artifact size, composition, surface morphology, heat retention, and other physical, chemical, and biological properties
Visibility	The extent to which an observer can detect the presence of archaeological materials at or below a given place	Site area, artifact density, artifact size, surface area of exposure, frequency of exposure
Accessibility	The effort required to reach a particular place	Climate, biotic environment, terrain, roads, landholding patterns

Information from Schiffer, Sullivan, and Klinger, 1978.

is a semiarid environment with little natural vegetation, an optimal condition for artifact and site location. It is heavily populated today, largely by village agriculturalists, and is crisscrossed by numerous roads. The characteristics of the environment and of modern land use facilitate archaeological work, and a record of continuous occupation for more than 20,000 years has been recovered. Small camps and animal kill sites (neither containing many tools) of simple hunting-gathering bands are present in fair number. More abundant and conspicuous are the urban centers with massive public architecture that characterize the complex societies of the Aztecs and their predecessors. By contrast, the nearly impenetrable lowland rainforests are not populous, extensively cultivated, or developed in any major way; consequently, they have few roads. Remains from earlier than 3000 B.C. are rare and the ceremonial centers of the Mayan civilization, though abundant, are clustered, nearly invisible, and practically inaccessible. Archaeological knowledge of the Highland and Lowland Mexico civilizations is unbalanced because of the radically different discovery probabilities. Research in the areas requires fundamentally different approaches.

Low discovery probability can be overcome in several ways. The sampling universe can be adjusted, the intensity of investigation can be increased, or the techniques of examination can be altered. In cases of clustered data, if the clustering is a known factor, the sampling universe can be designed to examine similar localities. For example, if sites of a given period cluster at stream confluences, and are seldom found elsewhere, the survey can be altered to examine all such places, or a fraction of them, determined by probability methods. Where sites, artifacts, or features are rare, crew size can be increased, spacing can be decreased, and the pace slowed to increase chances of encountering the rare data. Low visibility often can be overcome by deliberately plowing fields to expose artifacts, or by digging backhoe troughs, shovel, or auger test holes to locate materials. Remote sensing (e.g., aerial photography) and chemical testing also can be employed to overcome these problems.

Site Survey

In its most common form, archaeological survey has as its objective the location of archaeological sites. Dense artifact clusters are given primary attention, and unclustered artifacts and low-density clusters are excluded from systematic treatment. While site survey is conducted within clearly defined grid units (in a master system), the basic unit of observation and recording is the space defined by the distribution of artifacts forming a dense cluster. The product of a site survey is a set of site survey forms, and the discussion in this section is organized around the categories of information that are included on this form.

Since the objectives of a site survey vary widely depending on the problem under investigation, it is impossible to design a universal format for the site survey form. However, most forms do include information of a fairly standard sort. A list of these information categories is given in Table 5.2. Under each category, more specific observations are noted. An example of a general purpose form, used by the Ohio Archaeological Council to maintain a master catalog of archaeological sites in the state, is shown in Figure 5.1. A more detailed, special purpose form developed for use on a settlement pattern survey by the Chevelon Project in Arizona is shown in Figure 5.2.

Site designation. At the time of discovery, a site usually is given a numerical designation that is specific to the survey. Upon completion of the

Table 5.2. Categories of Information for Site Survey Forms

General Category	Specific Information
1. Site designation	Number, name, previous designations
2. Site location	Political unit (state, county, city, or town, township) Map coordinates (latitude and longitude, Universal Transverse Mercator, township-range) Verbal description
3. Previous investigation	Professional, amateur, vandalism
4. Ownership	Present owner, previous owner, tenants Attitude toward intensive investigation
5. Environment description	General environment (vegetation and soil zones, drainage system, landforms) Specific environment (flora, soil, slope, elevation, hydrology) Present land use (cultivation, housing, pasture, etc.)
6. Archaeological description	Artifacts observed and collected Dimensions (surface area and depth) Structure (surface concentrations and stratification) Relation to other sites
7. Cultural classification age estimate	Ethnic affiliation of recent occupants Cultural tradition, phase, or period Time period Function
8. Survey method	Personnel (field workers, record keepers) Sponsor (individual, organization, institution) Date of visit(s) Informants Survey conditions
9. References	Artifact catalog Photographs Field notebook pages Published references
10. Evaluation	Condition of site; recommendation for future intensive investigation
11. Map	Small-scale of area with site location marked Large-scale showing specific features of site

OHIO ARCHAEOLOGICAL INVENTORY

Ohio Archaeological Council
Ohio Historic Preservation Office
Ohio Historical Center
Columbus, Ohio 43211

1. Site Number	4. Site Name	
2. County	5. Other Names For Site	
3. Township		

6. City or Town Vicinity of ☐	14. Land Form	23. Ownership: Public ☐ Private ☐
7. Map Reference	15. Elevation	
	16. Soil Type	24. Form Prepared by
8. Township & Range Number	17. Floral Cover	
9. Section Number	18. Condition of Site	25. Organization
10. Latitude	19. Present Use	
11. Longitude	20. Type of Site	26. Location of Negatives
12. U.T.M. Reference		
Zone Easting Northing	21. Drainage System	27. Date of Survey
13. Verbal Site Location	22. Dimensions of Site	28. Survey Conditions
		29. Cultural Classification or Time Period

30. Artifacts Collected

31. References

32. Remarks

33. Use opposite side to copy portion of topographic map with site located, attachment of contact print, sketch of site plan, or continuation of items 1-32.

(right margin labels: 1. Site No   2. County   4. Site Name   5. Other Names for Site)

Figure 5.1. Archaeological Site Survey Form used by the Ohio Historic Preservation Office. This form was constructed for the purpose of compiling an inventory of archaeological sites in Ohio. It requires only general information on a site's archaeological characteristics and relationship to environmental features.

1. Site number CS-_____

2. ____1/4 of the ____ 1/4 of Section ____ of Range ____, Township ____

3. ____ degrees, ____minutes, ____ seconds longitude

4. ____ degrees, ____ minutes, ____ seconds latitude

5. Description of site location:

6. Owner of property _____

7. Damage by pothunters: a. one hole b. several holes c. extensive

8. Damage by erosion: a. little b. some c. substantial d. total

9. Access now; factors inhibiting access to artifacts, features:

10. Elevation _____

11. LPD Unit _____

12. Landform on which site is located _____

13. Landform unit in which site is located _____

14. Degrees of vision of at least 1 km. _____

15. Degrees of vision of at least 5 km. _____

16. Walking time to nearest water _____

17. Canopy: a. grass b. + bushes c. + low trees d. + high trees

18. Soil type on site _____

19. Predominant soil in vicinity _____

20. Plant "stand" in which site occurs _____

21. Other stands within 2 km. _____

22. Other stands within 10 km. _____

23. Plant community in which site occurs _____

24. Other communities within 2 km. _____

25. Other communities within 10 km. _____

Figure 5.2. Archaeological Site Form used by the Chevelon Survey, Arizona. The form is designed to provide information for the detailed investigation of prehistoric settlement pattern. (From "Chevelon archaeological research project," by Fred Plog, Figure 4. University of California Los Angeles, Department of Anthropology, Archaeological Survey, *Annual Report* 13:5-24. 1971.)

26. Acreage of arable land within 2 km. of site _____   ____

27. Nearest water source _____   Distance to it _____   ____

28. Mineral outcrops _____   Distance _____   ____

29. Total site area ____m^2; geometric form: N-S___, E-W___, 1 other ___   ____

30. Pottery: a. absent   b. 0-10   c. 10-100   d. 100-1000   e. +1000   ____

31. Chipped stone: a. absent   b. 0-10   c. 10-100   d. 100-1000   e. +1000   ____

32. Ground stone: a. absent   b. 0-10   c. 10-100   d. 100-1000   e. +1000   ____

33. Activity features present ____ absent ____   ____

34. List features if present _____,_____, _____,   ____

    _____,_____,_____,_____

35. Pithouses: present____ absent ____; number actually observable ____   ____

36. Pueblos: present ____ absent ____; number of rooms actually observable ____   ____

37. Area of house mounds or depressions: ____m^2 (____m x ____m)   ____

38. If pueblo, height of rubble mound ____m.   ____

39. Identifiable burial ground _____   ____

40. Irrigation channels: present ____ absent ____   ____

41. Terraces: present ____ absent ____   ____

42. Linear grids: present ____ absent ____   ____

43. Linear borders: present ____ absent ____   ____

44. If water control feature, slope of land to which water carried ____%   ____

45. If water control feature, soil of land to which water carried ____%   ____

46. Slope ____%   ____

47. Exposure ____ degrees to ____ degrees   ____

48. Depth of midden _____   ____

49. Photos: no. ____ of roll ____; no. ____ of roll ____; no. ____ of roll ____   ____

50. Form recorded by:_____   51.   Site mapped by: _____   ____

52. Report checked by: _____   _53.   Coded by: _____   ____

54. Keypunched by: _____   ____

55. Site dated to: _____   56.   Site type _____   ____

Further Comments:

Figure 5.2—*Continued.*

project, however, designations in a more comprehensive system are assigned to each of the discovered sites. In the United States, a system that originated in Illinois was adopted in the 1940s by the Smithsonian Institution River Basin Survey program and has become standard in nearly all states. This system assigns a numerical code for the state, a two-letter code for county, and a serial number for each site. For example, 33-FR-58 refers to the 58th site recorded in Franklin (FR) County, Ohio. Ohio in this case is the 33rd state in an alphabetical list of states, excluding Alaska and Hawaii.

In addition to a numerical or alphabetical designation, sites often are given names. When dealing with a large number of sites, archaeologists find it easier to remember names than numbers. In the United States sites are commonly given the last name of the property owner. This is done out of courtesy to the owner, since in most cases owners are not, or cannot be, compensated for their cooperation in permitting investigations on their land. Geographic place names, associated constructions, and landforms are other possibilities for a site name.

Quite often, sites that are being designated in a new system will have been assigned numbers in an older, probably nonuniform, system. Whenever this situation arises, it is necessary to record on a site survey form both the new and the old number to avoid confusion.

Site location. Although site designation systems give in coded form a certain amount of locational data, and in special cases might be designed to include exact global coordinates, on most site survey forms most or all of this information must also be written out. Thus spaces are provided for state and county and perhaps the nearest city and township. In addition to these units, one should note the precise coordinates in at least two of the following systems: latitude and longitude; Universal Transverse Mercator (UTM); and, where it exists in the United States, the Northwest Ordinance system of township, range, and section. The system actually used will depend on the presence of its grid units on the maps available for the area. Not all regions are covered by the Northwest Ordinance Survey, for example, nor do all maps include the UTM grids. Also, the more systems used, the more complete the locational data, since each has its own margin of error, and with several locational coordinates the chance of error is reduced.

Of the three coordinate systems named above, latitude and longitude has the advantage of existing on nearly all maps, regardless of age. This system offers a degree of accuracy that is sufficient for most archaeological purposes. Calculated to the nearest second of a degree, a point can be located within a circle of 30-meter (100-foot) diameter. The UTM system is more accurate and allows description of a point to within 10 meters of the actual point. Although it is on all recent editions of topographic maps published by the U.S. Geological Survey, it is not as widely used as the latitude and longitude system. Northwest Ordinance locations are the least accurate and the least universal of the group. The smallest practical measurement is the quarter-quarter-quarter section, an area one-eighth mile square, or plus or minus 203 meters (660 feet) of the actual point. This system, which was devised to regulate land ownership and exchange in the United States, does not include the eastern seaboard states. Moreover, the sections are often oddly shaped and the determination of successively smaller quarter sections becomes tortured in actual practice.

An example of the combined use of the UTM, latitude and longitude, and Northwest Ordinance systems is shown in Figure 5.3. (For a detailed explanation of the calculations, consult any text on surveying and mapping.) Two short articles by archaeologists (Edwards 1969; Dills 1970) discuss the pros and cons of the various systems and illustrate the use of the UTM system (Edwards 1969).

Our discussion has assumed an important point that may have already raised some questions in your mind. How do you know where you are on a map in order to plot a point subsequently described by the coordinate systems? Conversely, how do you transfer a point from the map to the ground in locating a site from its coordinates? In theory, the answer is simple. Use a compass or a more sophisticated surveying instrument, such as a transit, to triangulate the site from natural or cultural features of the landscape that are shown on the map. A water tower, the intersection of two roads, a house, or a barn are often visible from the site and appear as points on the map, as do mountain peaks, prominent rock outcrops, and other landforms. All these features can be used in triangulating site location. The process can be used to locate a site on a map as well as to pinpoint that site with coordinate data.

In practice, the procedure may prove difficult, especially in featureless terrain with few or no buildings or distinctive landforms. Here, one must use the full map to "eye-ball" the location and traverse the area until the kind of material recorded on the form is found by trial and error.

Hayes and Osborne (1961) describe a technique in which a radio-direction finder is used to fix site locations on featureless, undeveloped terrain. Their archaeological survey of Weatherill Mesa, Mesa Verde National Park, employed two low-power portable radio transmitters and a portable receiver to locate sites by triangulation. Producing signals readable at one-half mile, the transmitters were set up on reference points established by the archaeologists or already present on maps of the survey region. The signals differed in frequency and the receiver was rotated on a board with a movable compass rose until it aligned with the signal first of one and then the other transmitter. Hayes and Osborne estimate an accuracy of 20 meters (65 feet) for the method and it takes half the time of conventional methods.

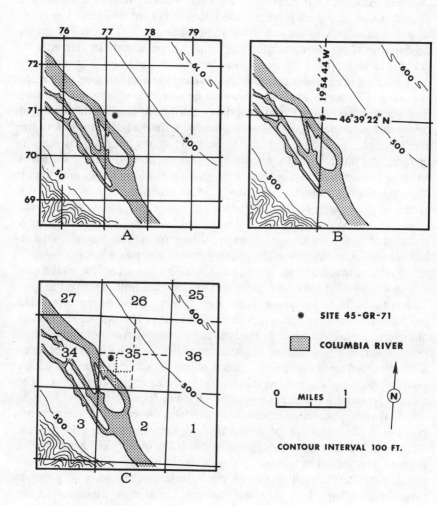

Figure 5.3. Three reference systems for recording site location. The location of Site 45-GR-71 in Grant County, Washington, on the Columbia River is shown in relation to the Universal Transverse Mercator system (A), geographical coordinates (B), and the Northwest Ordinance Survey system (C). The complete geographical coordinates are given in the figure. The complete reference in the UTM system is 11TKB772709 and for the Ordinance Survey it is NW¼ of the SW¼ of Section 35, Township 14N, Range 23E, Wilamette Meridian.

Before adoption of standard systems of designation and coordinate location of archaeological sites, written descriptions were employed exclusively. Although it is no substitute for the systems mentioned above, it is good practice to include a verbal description in the survey form. The coordinates and maps will get you to the right place, but it is helpful to have a description of the surroundings and some measurements in reference to landmarks to pinpoint the site. If the landmarks have not been moved or defaced, they are handier reference points than the abstract lines on a map.

Map. Of course no site form would be complete without a map. One might be drawn from the locational data described in detail in the form, but this verbal information cannot substitute for a field-made map. Before the survey begins, a decision will have to be made as to what mapping scale to use and how much detail to include. For some purposes it may be sufficient to trace the general terrain from a large-scale published map and simply show the map as a dot on that tracing. Most often, the best map will be a sketch of the specific features of the site, its landforms, buildings, adjacent roads, and so on. Drawn originally in the field notebook, it is subsequently transferred to the back page of the site survey form. The map should also include the locations of surface collections and test pits when relevant.

Previous investigation. On occasion, and in some areas frequently, sites will be located that have been excavated at an earlier time. This fact may be known through the literature of the area or from traces of the excavation pits and trenches. Increasingly, vandals have taken chunks out of a newly discovered site. Even in areas thought to be remote from nonprofessional penetration, it is not unusual to come upon disorderly backdirt piles laden with discarded tools and debris. This problem is becoming worse as leisure time increases and rugged recreational vehicles become more common. The extent of vandalism should be noted on the site form.

Ownership. Accurate determination of land ownership is extremely important in the reporting of archaeological site information. In no case should land be entered without permission. If the owner does not reside on the land, this should be indicated, along with the name and address of possible tenants. An attempt should be made to learn the names of previous owners and tenants. They may be able to provide information on collections from the site and changing land use patterns for the area that can aid in evaluation of the site's potential and condition. Since it may be desirable to return for more intensive investigation, effort should be made to ascertain the owner's and the tenant's attitude toward additional work. It would be a tragic oversight to plan a program of excavation or intensive surface examination and then learn that the owner is hostile to archaeology.

Environment description. Description of the general surroundings of a site and its specific environmental characteristics is necessary for correct evaluation of its condition and for examination of site location preferences in preliminary analysis of survey data. For the general picture, the soil, vegetation, drainage, and landforms of the site can be listed. An important part of planning a survey is the acquisition of maps of zonal associations for the survey region. These can be consulted in the field or in camp for relevant data. Information of a more specific nature should also be included. What is the soil like, the lay of the land, the elevation, the relation to streams, rivers, springs, or other sources of water? How accessible is the site from roads or natural avenues of travel? Is erosion active on the site? Might past erosion have affected use of the locality and the condition of the site? In addition, notes on present and past land use should be included. It is important to know whether the site is currently under cultivation and, if so, which plants are grown and in what rotation cycle. Has the land been modified from its original contour? Have buildings been removed? What is the history of the site from the standpoint of its use by recent occupants?

Although one could write endlessly about the environmental characteristics of a site, the point is to include enough data so that the site and its setting can be visualized from only the site survey form and maps.

Archaeological description. The kinds of artifacts observed or collected in the process of surveying should be recorded. Also essential are an estimate of the dimensions of the site based on surface-exposed artifact distribution and notes on soil discoloration and natural landform limitations. The depth of artifacts and the presence or absence of cultural stratification are an important part of a description. Surface concentrations should also be noted since they give clues to the horizontal structure of the site and may be important in determining the nature of the occupation and the priority of the site for future examination. Comments can be added about the proximity of the site to other sites so that the form itself, without additional compilation of data, conveys a picture of the clustering of sites in the immediate area.

Cultural classification and age estimate. An estimation of the cultural tradition, phase, or period of a site is essential for analysis and planning. Ethnographic maps of tribal or other ethnic group distributions can be consulted to determine the identity of the most recent aboriginal or indigenous inhabitants. Classification and age estimates will be based on the styles of artifacts collected by the surveyor or seen in collections acquired by the landowner, tenant, or local amateur collectors. The collections and surface features of the site may also permit speculation about the function of the site. Does it appear to have been a hunting camp, an agricultural village, a quarry, or some other element of the settlement system?

Comments on method. A site survey form is not complete until it includes some information about how the site was found, by whom, under whose sponsorship, on what date, and under what conditions. Since it may be necessary to contact the individuals responsible for filing the report, the names of the field workers, the person completing the form, and the organization or institution sponsoring the survey should be noted. If a local resident or other archaeologist has directed the field workers to the site, the informant's name should be given. The general conditions of discovery may be deduced from the date of the survey, but additional information on the weather, the amount of time spent on the site, the ability of the field workers to cover the ground, and other factors affecting the accuracy of observations of the site's characteristics should be given. It is also desirable to include a statement about collection and testing procedures. If artifacts are collected and removed, is the process selective or total, purposive or randomized? Are test pits excavated, and if so what are their locations, surface dimensions, and depths?

Records and references. The site forms will be completed from field notebooks containing the relevant information in greater detail than is given on the forms. Reference should be made to the notebook pages so that information on the forms can be checked if necessary, or so that someone using the forms can refer to the notebooks for more information. Collected artifacts will be listed, and if a summary of this list is not given in the site form, reference can be made to the list. The relevant roll and exposure numbers of photographs taken should appear on the form. If previous investigations of an intensive survey have been performed and the results published, it is useful to give the relevant bibliographic citations. In short, the survey form should indicate as briefly as possible the kinds of additional information and records that exist about the site, giving references so records can be found and consulted if necessary.

Evaluation. When summarizing the various kinds of information gathered on a site, it is worthwhile to make a brief statement about the condition of the site. Have erosion patterns or modern land use destroyed or altered the site? What potential does the site have for future, more intensive investigation? Comments on these matters may be of only passing interest to someone using the survey information for distributional studies, but in most cases surveys are initiated to locate sites with excavation possibilities, or potential for intensive surface collection. In such cases, a brief evaluation of this sort by the field worker is imperative.

Intensive Examination of Site Surfaces

In the conduct of a site survey, the degree of precision with which surface characteristics of a site are noted and mapped varies widely. At one extreme is the brief notation based on a casual, unsystematic inspection. At the other extreme is an intensive, systematic examination to obtain a detailed picture of the boundaries and surface structure of a site. The pattern that emerges can be used alone for comparative study of various sites in a region, or help plan the location of test pits and full-scale excavation of a single site. In the following paragraphs we will look at examples of intensive recording of surface-exposed artifacts, soil testing, and geophysical prospecting which, although sensing and measuring subsurface features, is basically a method of intensive surface examination.

Surface collection. One of the most obvious sources of information on site configuration and internal structure is the distribution of surface-exposed artifacts. Surface distributions offer an approximate idea of site boundaries while surface densities can provide clues to localization of past activities within a site. Tool type analysis of the surface-exposed implements sketches a picture of the activities carried out in the various sections of a site. Analysis of pottery and tool styles can indicate the general age of a deposit and suggest the number of distinct occupations in cases where a site has been intermittently used by culturally different populations. Settlements are not always stationary and frequently migrate laterally as older sections are abandoned and new housing and other structures are built. Surface data can be informative about this type of internal variation as well.

The intensive surface collection of Hatchery West (Fig. 5.4) on the east bank of the Kaskaskia River, southern Illinois, in 1963 (Binford et al. 1970), although not the first example of this kind of research, certainly has been the most influential, and much subsequent work has been modeled after it. Hatchery West is a multicomponent site occupied primarily in the Late Woodland Period between A.D. 250 and A.D. 800. The surface examination was designed to determine the boundaries of the site and to recover artifacts which in combination with excavated features could be used to analyze the internal structure of the site.

The field work at Hatchery West proceeded as follows. After photographing the site from the air for planning purposes, archaeologists plowed the surface to enhance the exposure of artifacts. On completion of the plowing, they staked out a grid system of units 6 meters (20 feet) square. Each of the 416 squares was totally collected by a base crew of 11 persons in a four-day period after rain had washed the exposed material. The distribution and density of the 7817 items (including stone tools and manufacturing debris, pottery sherds, bones, shells, and introduced limestone, sandstone, and cobbles) recovered in this 1.5-hectare (3.69-acre) area were analyzed for patterns. Using the limits of sherd distribution as the boundaries of the site, and after hand excavation of several large blocks in areas of concentrated surface material, they stripped off the plowed zone with a roadgrader and a bulldozer-pulled scoop. The new surface was then gridded and covered with plastic to retard drying. Square by square, features were located, mapped, and excavated. Among the several hundred features present were house floors, earth ovens, cooking pits, and rock hearths.

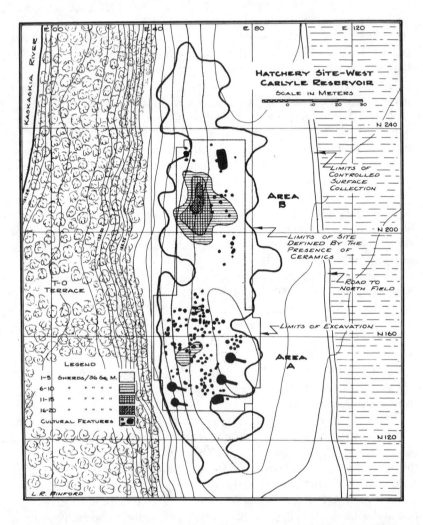

Figure 5.4. Site plan of the Hatchery West Site, Illinois. The general configuration of the site was determined by plotting the distribution of ceramic sherds. Houses, storage pits, and other cultural features were located by excavation. (Reproduced from Binford et al. 1970 by permission of The Society for American Archaeology from *Memoirs of the SAA* 24:5.)

Hatchery West is an example of an exhaustive collection of surface material. The experience points out that surface material is patterned in a meaningful way and that the study of surface-exposed material can hasten the objectives of complete community exposure. Inspired by the results at this Midwestern American site, Redman and Watson (1970) used a similar approach in the investigation of the Çayönü Site in Turkey. Departing somewhat from the Hatchery model, these archaeologists employed probability sampling to obtain a partial sample. Their purpose also differed in that they employed the surface collection to aid in the placement of small excavation units.

Çayönü (Fig 5.5) is a Neolithic *tell*, or village mound, occupied about 7000 B.C., that rises 4 meters (13 feet) above the average level of the plain where it is located. It covers an area of about 2.5 hectares (6 acres) and has been plowed with draft animals and wooden plow for several thousand years. A surface collection was initiated by establishing a 5-meter-interval grid over the mound. Artifacts were collected from 75 randomly selected squares to obtain a 10 percent sample of the abundant lithic, bone, and ceramic artifacts on the site.

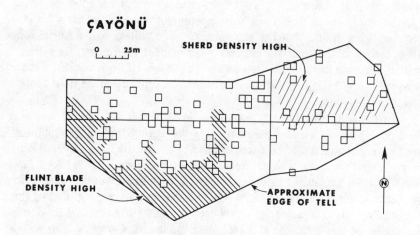

ÇAYÖNÜ

0   25m

SHERD DENSITY HIGH

FLINT BLADE
DENSITY HIGH

APPROXIMATE
EDGE OF TELL

N

Figure 5.5. Controlled surface collection of Çayönü, Turkey. The sampling units shown are 5 meters square and represent a 10 percent random sample of the site. Analysis of the recovered artifacts revealed that ceramic sherds were densest in the northeast quadrant of the site and flint blades were densest in the southwest quadrant. A general picture of the internal structure of the site was thus derived from the systematic, intensive surface collection. (Adapted from Redman and Watson 1970)

One pattern found in the Çayönü surface collection was a concentration of pottery at one end of the mound and a cluster of flint blades at the opposite end. Excavation confirmed this distribution and supported the investigators' suspicion that the sherd-strewn area was occupied during a later period than the rest of the site. Differences in the quantity of debris per 5-meter square suggested another pattern in which open and enclosed areas of the village might be reflected in the surface collection. Excavation of low density areas produced evidence of structures which were absent in the areas with a high density of surface debris.

Another approach to intensive examination of site surfaces through surface collection of artifacts is illustrated by work in 1972 at a site in Missouri called the Hopper Site (23-BO-1A). Lacking the time to perform either a total pickup or a randomly based partial collection of all classes of surface-exposed material, the director devised an alternative method (Chomko 1974). Preliminary to an intensive surface collection, archaeologists searched 0.74 hectare (1.8 acres) of the site for diagnostic artifacts. Working within a grid of 31-meter (100-foot) squares, they located and mapped tools, ornaments, and pottery sherds. They marked artifact locations with color-coded polyethelene flags 8 centimeters (3 inches) square attached to wires 0.6 meter (2 feet) long and 0.1 centimeter (¹⁄₁₆ inch) in diameter; yellow flags signified ceramics and white marked stone tools. Upon completion of the survey, they examined the maps and flags for patterning. They found that the site consisted of a village and a burial area (Fig. 5.6) and that activity clusters were evident in the surface-exposed material. Subsequently, they examined select areas of both site districts intensively to obtain more detailed information on the nature of the site's structure.

Intensive surface collection of a site in Mexico in 1973 by Tolstoy and Fish (1975) provides one more example of the method and additional information on the nature of surface deposits. The investigation centered on a portion of Coapexco, a site thought to have been occupied between 1150 B.C. and 1100 B.C. and to represent one of the earliest known sedentary communities in the Basin of Mexico. A one-hectare (2.5-acre) segment of this large 50-hectare (125-acre) site was chosen for study. In preparing for a total collection of this area, the archaeologists made a topographic map with a contour interval of 25 centimeters (10 inches) and staked out 572 contiguous grid units each 4 meters (13 feet) square. All materials in 489 of the squares were collected, and sherds, figurines, and chipped stone tools were recovered in an additional 36 squares. The work was undertaken to obtain data on population size and community structure, so the surface collections were designed to locate the site's boundaries, density variations within the

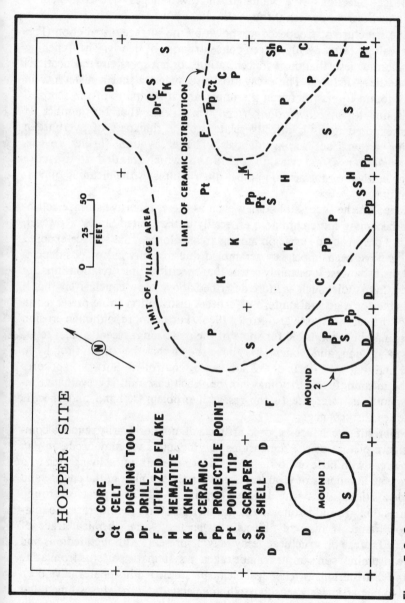

Figure 5.6. Controlled surface collection of the Hopper Site, Missouri. By recording the exact locations of tools on the surface, archaeologists could reconstruct the layout of a portion of the village. (Adapted from Chomko 1974)

site, and qualitative differences between concentrations. After the results of the surface collections were evaluated, shallow trenches were excavated by hand in a crisscross pattern through the site.

The structure of Coapexco as shown by the surface distribution (Fig. 5.7) reveals 53 fairly evenly spaced concentrations of debris. The trenching excavation suggests that these concentrations, or hot spots, are the locations of domestic structures. The excavation also suggests that a difference in density found to exist between the upper and lower parts of the sampled area is due to an *attenuation effect*. This means that the number of surface-exposed items is directly related to the thickness of overburden covering an artifact-bearing deposit. The excavation further reveals that a *merger effect* was in operation which tended to obscure through cultivation the actual number of structures by the blending of concentrations.

Based on the success of studies such as these, intensive surface collection is becoming more common, especially in the United States. However, there is a deep-rooted suspicion among archaeologists that surface-exposed artifacts have been hopelessly scrambled due to a myriad of postdepositional disturbances. It certainly is true that specific artifact relationships are lacking, but studies such as those described above show conclusively that it is possible for a general pattern of artifact distribution to be preserved in spite of displacement (see also Roper 1976). Furthermore, although erosion factors may be responsible for some of the patterning, recent studies (e.g., Fuchs, Kaufman, and Ronen 1977) have shown that they are not totally to blame and that the effects of erosion can be controlled. Surface exposures may be meaningful or they may not be. Each case must be evaluated independently in reference to the research problem at hand and specific sources of disturbance.

Soil testing. Surface-exposed artifacts do not necessarily render a comprehensive picture of site dimensions and layout. They may occur only in dump areas with little or no surface evidence present in the living area of a settlement. Standards of cleanliness may have been high in the culture and past depositional decay rapid. However, human use of a piece of ground modifies that ground in one way or another and leaves some trace, no matter how faint. If discrete objects are lacking, some chemical trace of discarded refuse or structural decay may be present. Although tedious and time-consuming, soil samples can be taken in systematic patterns from a site and the distributions of chemical elements studied. Phosphates have been found to be particularly sensitive to human activity; it may be assumed that soils with high phosphate levels have been heavily used by human groups (Cook and Heizer 1956; Eidt 1973). The source of an abnormal phosphate

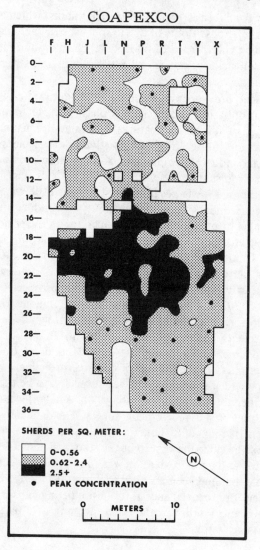

Figure 5.7. Controlled surface collection of Coapexco, Mexico. The density of ceramic sherds, collected in 4-meter-square units, revealed a definite structure. Of particular interest are the peak concentrations of sherds and associated figurine parts, chipped stone items, and various kinds of grinding stones. Excavations of a sample of these concentrations produced evidence of domestic structures. (Adapted from Tolstoy and Fish 1975)

level is usually food refuse (bones, meat, fish, plants) which can accumulate in a village and on house floors of dirt in spite of strict adherence to external garbage dumping rules. Maps of phosphate, calcium, and nitrogen concentration, and soil acidity, can reveal much about the structure of an archaeological site.

Geophysical prospecting. Another method of intensive surface examination is geophysical prospecting (Coles 1972). Of many devices that permit mapping of subsurface features from measurements at the surface, two basic types are in use. Electrical resistivity devices measure differences in the electrical conductivity of the soil. A stone structure foundation below the surface in a moist soil, for example, presents a distinct pattern of high resistivity readings. This is because the stone has little water compared to the soil and consequently has a lower ability to conduct an electrical current. Another set of prospecting devices operates on the principle of thermoremanent magnetism, whereby the magnetic properties of matter are altered as a result of heating and cooling. Disturbed earth in trenches, pits, or other constructions, as well as heated materials such as pottery, pottery kilns, bricks, and hearths, can be detected by magnetic prospected devices.

Glenn Black (Black and Johnston 1962) of Indiana University tested the use of proton magnetometry in detecting stockade walls and house floors in a sixteenth-century Indian town on the Ohio River upstream from Evansville, Indiana, known today as Angel Mounds. A low, narrow ridge around the periphery of the site was discovered through excavation to be the remains of a wooden stockade. An area suspected to be the location of an earlier stockade, erected when the village was smaller, was intersected in a number of places by a magnetometry survey. The data showed two parallel linear patterns of magnetic anomalies, one of which corresponded to the topography of the ridge thought to be the stockade line. The second pattern was unexpected and upon excavation was found to represent the course of a recent field tile that had been installed to drain the land for farming. The instrument, therefore, proved successful in predicting subsurface remains of cultural significance, although the exact meaning of a pattern may not be clear without excavation.

Nonsite Survey

As noted earlier, the archaeological site is the fundamental unit of observation and recording in most survey work. Although site is often defined as the location of any trace of past human activity, in reality sites usually consist of concentrations of artifacts marking the location of settlements or intensive activity loci. Site surveys generally are not concerned with the low-density scatter of artifacts that are present between the concentrations. While site survey data are well suited to the problems of the organizational and developmental characteristics of human groups, they are inadequate for investigations of the prehistoric utilization of the environment as a whole. For problems of the latter sort, an approach referred to as the "nonsite survey" (Thomas 1974) has emerged.

In contrast to the site survey, the objective of a nonsite survey is to recover all kinds of information on the human use of space, not just sites. Attention is directed to the total environment and field workers are encouraged to adopt a more comprehensive view of artifact distribution than is possible with the concept of site. Used alone, or in combination with site survey, nonsite survey can be an important data recovery method for the investigation of questions of subsistence change.

The method of a nonsite survey differs little from the site survey in the early stages of design. A survey region is selected in reference to a problem and its derivative hypotheses. The region is partitioned on an environmental basis, preferably topographic since variables like vegetation are notoriously unstable. Sampling units are defined which assure adequate representation of the environmental and microenvironmental variation present in the region. It is at this point that the two approaches diverge, for the recovery requirements of the nonsite survey are different from those of the site survey.

In its most rigorous form, nonsite survey calls for the exact location of all items within the sampling unit. The notation of exact locations for each item rather than for groups of items, as in site survey, requires greater control over the coverage of a unit and more time for actual inspection of the surface. Sampling units, therefore, must be selected with greater deliberation because fewer units can be covered in a comparable amount of time in contrast to a site survey. Furthermore, the units must be relatively small to permit the locational precision required by the approach, but large enough to sample the relevant environmental variation.

When exact location of all items is desired, the field work proceeds in the following manner. The sampling unit, transect or quadrat, is established by marking its corners and perhaps also its borders. Provided with some means of assuring regularity in their traverses, the field workers move from one end of the unit to the other. As artifacts are encountered, they are either marked for recording and collected upon completion of the unit or they are recorded and collected on the spot. The advantage of the former is that, with all locations marked, perhaps with brightly colored flags coded for artifact type, the distributional pattern within the unit can be directly perceived upon completion of the unit. If the contrast with the ground is sufficiently great, a photographic record of the distribution can be obtained. Also, since methods of locational mapping differ in speed and accuracy, it may be advantageous to postpone recording until the magnitude of the surveying and mapping job is known. Then an appropriate method can be selected to maximize recording efficiency.

A common deviation from exact location is the use of grid location in cases where concentrations are encountered. The precise recording of each of thousands of items lying side by side or piled on one another strains the accuracy of the measuring instruments and is inordinately time-consuming. Moreover, it is doubtful that the information of exact locations in these cases would be useful. In the place of exact locations, then, unit locations within a grid system can be used. The size of the units will depend on the size and density of the scatter, but as in excavation, the optimal unit size probably lies between one and 5 meters square.

The exact and small-unit grid location of artifacts means that nonsite survey data has the potential of dealing with sites, perhaps even in a more precise manner than can be done with the results of a site survey. Since artifacts are recorded irrespective of their clustering in settlements, exact or nearly exact locational data is available for all material in a recovery unit. If settlement pattern is part of a problem initiating a nonsite survey, the locational data can be analyzed in terms of item density or spacing, and sites with objective definitions can be demarcated within the general distribution of artifacts. Thus, although "siteless" in its recovery tactics, a nonsite survey can generate sites from its data.

An extreme form of nonsite survey exists in which no exact locations are recorded. Here, artifacts are collected and recorded within some large-scale unit. In the example from Oaxaca, Mexico, summarized below, agricultural plots were adopted as the basic collection unit and sherds of a certain type were collected within these units without regard for their exact location. The decision of which extreme to use is dependent on the problem, and most nonsite surveys will achieve various degrees of locational exactness for various artifact classes.

It should be understood that along with item location, recording, and collection, or prior to it, information on the environmental context must be obtained. Variations in exposure visibility and obtrusiveness are highly important in large-scale surface work, and analysis of artifact distribution must be able to take this into account. Otherwise, distributional patterns which may be the result of differential exposure or erosion may be mistaken for patterns of human activity.

Davis (1975) describes a project in California which, although not identified as such, is a classic example of nonsite survey. The work took place in the desert environment of a portion of the Indian Wells Valley known as China Lake. It was initiated to collect information on the problem of whether Paleo-Indian projectile point styles in the area represent different populations or different activities performed by groups of essentially the same people. Lanceolate points and stemmed points, although conceded to belong to the same cultural tradition, have long been thought to represent different phases of development in time. Davis considered it equally possible that the points were contemporary and that they were part of a diversified tool kit in use by persons of a single interacting social unit. Guiding the work was the idea that repeated association of the point styles in the same surface clusters would support the view of tool kit differences while separation in space would support the distinct populations hypothesis.

The China Lake research design is too elaborate to summarize completely, but the manner in which the surface-exposed items were located and mapped can be described in isolation to illustrate the technical aspects of nonsite survey (Fig. 5.8). Before the selection of specific sampling units, the area was scouted, or reconnoitered, to gain familiarity with its exposure patterns of artifacts and faunal material. After the scouting was completed, field workers erected stakes at select locations and established square sampling units around the stakes. They placed steel rods at the corners of these units and at the midpoints of their boundaries so that the squares, which usually measured approximately 300 meters (975 feet) on a side, could be divided into quadrants. The borders were made visible by dragging stadia rods between the steel rods, thus creating a "drag line." After demarcating the survey unit, they mapped the internal vegetation, sediments, and soil patterns.

The actual work of locating artifacts was accomplished by pedestrian traverses one to 1.5 meters (4 to 5 feet) apart and marked by drag lines as the work proceeded. Tools and bones were numbered, mapped, and collected as they were encountered. Each field worker carried a stadia rod, which was used to produce the drag line. When an artifact or bone was located, it was numbered and its location sighted from a plane-table and alidade station erected over the central stake; then the item was collected and bagged. Each field worker carried a packet of 8-by-5 punch cards on which recorded the date, the field worker's name, the quad, the stake, the serial code for the item, and its distance from the central datum stake. A description and drawing of the item, and a description of the physical setting of the find spot, were included as well. In short, a minisurvey form was

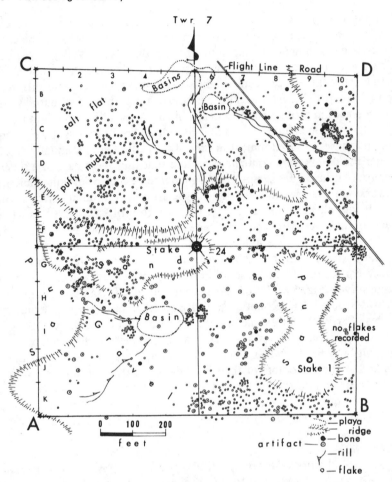

Figure 5.8. Nonsite survey at China Lake, California. Precise recording of item locations enabled detailed study of item clustering and the associations of various classes of artifacts in this and other sampling units. (Reproduced from Davis 1975 by permission of The Society for American Archaeology from *American Antiquity* 40(1):48.)

completed for each tool and bone located by the survey. Flakes were collected and recorded in less precise fashion. Information on the general location of flake clusters and descriptive information on the setting was recorded on a separate set of punch cards. The flakes were bagged without regard for the exact location of each one.

Mason, Lewarch, O'Brien, and Neely (1977) describe a nonsite survey in which no exact locations were recorded. The work took place in Oaxaca, Mexico, near the site of Monte Alban. Monte Alban is the largest site in the Valley of Oaxaca and was one of several centers of cultural development in Mesoamerica during the Formative Period (1150 B.C. to A.D. 250). It is situated on a series of hilltops, and below it on the Xoxocotlan Piedmont is a prehistoric dam and associated canal which have been dated to the Late Formative (550 to 400 B.C.). Mason and associates were interested in the role this system of hydraulic agriculture may have had in the growth of Monte Alban. This settlement, which was approaching the status of a city, presumably was importing a sizeable portion of its food, and the nearby canal area was a prime candidate as a source of agricultural products. In pursuing this question, they decided that field research was needed to establish the amount of arable land in relation to land occupied by settlements of the period along the canal or within the boundaries of the plateau through which it coursed.

The study area was defined as the surface of the ridge which could have been irrigated by the canal, an area with maximum dimensions of 2000 by 400 meters (6500 by 1300 feet) (Fig. 5.9). The presence of small agricultural plots of approximately the same size obviated the need for an artificial grid system. The fields, which were numbered, became the collection units. Each field was covered on foot in traverses spaced at 3-meter (10-foot) intervals. Although most fields contained large quantities of sherds, only rim sherds were collected. This selection was made because dating the period of occupation or utilization was of paramount importance to the project. Rims in this area, as in most others with ceramic populations, are the most sensitive to stylistic change and offer data in reference to regionally standardized typologies. Collection of only rim sherds also shortened collection time. Along with the rim sherd collection, notes were recorded on the type of vegetation and the amount of surface exposure for each field. This information was necessary to adjust density figures on sherd distribution to reflect differences in sherd visibility from field to field.

Analyzing the Xoxocotlan data on sherd densities, archaeologists found that after the subtraction of slopes and residential areas from the universe, the total arable land during the period in question amounted to approximately 50 hectares (125 acres). This amount of land was about what would have been needed to feed the populations of the immediate area; little surplus would have been available to divert to Monte Alban. Strengthening the likelihood of local consumption, a pattern of settlement size increase was found in the study area. The area of residential settlement increased from 2.5 hectares (6 acres) in Early Monte Alban I (550 to 400 B.C.) to 10.2 hectares (25 acres) in Late Monte Alban I (400 to 150 B.C.).

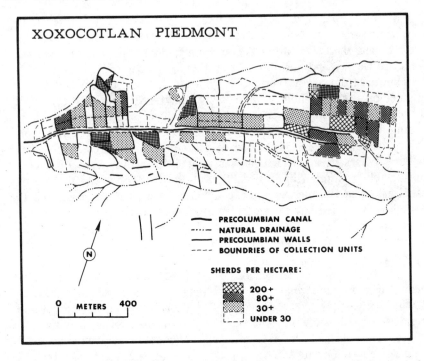

Figure 5.9. Nonsite survey on the Xoxocotlan Piedmont, Mexico. Collection of rim sherds from ceramic vessels within the field system of this study area revealed the pattern of prehistoric settlement along an irrigation canal in the vicinity of the prehistoric site of Monte Alban. (Adapted from Mason et al. 1977)

Aerial Photography

Aerial photography is a tool of inestimable value to archaeological survey. A bird's-eye view of a landscape gives a perspective on cultural and natural patterns and their articulation unattainable from the ground. Furthermore, traces of human activity invisible or imperceptible from the ground can often be seen clearly from the air. Sites can be located, outlines of structures can be seen, transportation routes and irrigation canals can be traced across the landscape, and abandoned field systems can be identified. Some of these patterns can be seen immediately with the naked eye, but usually careful study is necessary for detection. Often the patterns and traces are not within the normal range of human vision, and it is therefore necessary to have photographic images of the terrain to take full advantage of the benefits of an aerial view.

Aerial photographs can be taken from towers, balloons, aircraft, and satellites. The camera can be hand-held or remote controlled. Photographs can be made at an oblique angle, but vertical angles are the most useful for archaeological purposes. Photographs taken from an aircraft, with remote-controlled timed exposures, provide overlapping images which permit stereoscopic viewing.

Panchromatic films are the most common medium of aerial photography. They depict a subject in shades of gray, in the range of spectral sensitivity suited to the human eye. Normal color films enhance separation of tonal differences and therefore can be more useful than black-and-white panchromatic images for many subjects. Differences in vegetation and bodies of water are brought out most clearly in films which include or are limited to the infrared portion of the color spectrum. Panchromatic infrared and color infrared (false-color) films are quite useful in archaeological studies when archaeological remains have had an effect on vegetation patterns and on the moisture-retaining properties of a soil.

Existing photographs can be obtained from government agencies or private firms. Black-and-white imagery from low-altitude flights is available for all of the United States from one or a combination of the following agencies: Agricultural Stabilization and Conservation Service; Soil Conservation Service; Forest Service; Geological Survey; Army Corps of Engineers; Air Force; and National Ocean Survey.

Although existing photographs have not been acquired with archaeological purposes in mind, the high cost of original flights, especially for regional coverage, forces reliance on what is already available. Fortunately, agency concerns and archaeological purposes often coincide, as in hydrological, geological, forest, and crop studies, and most archaeological objectives can be accomplished with existing imagery. Only in special cases is the expense of a special flight necessary. The most troublesome problem is that the photographs may not have been taken at the time of year when they would be most useful to archaeologists. For instance, archaeological purposes might be best served by photographs taken in the spring and fall, when vegetation is sprouting or dying; but the photographs available may have been made in the summer for the purpose of detecting and mapping diseased vegetation during the season of maximum growth.

The use of aerial photographs for the detection and recording of archaeological features is based on the principle that photo examination must begin with the identification of general environmental patterns. To be sure, human use of the earth has brought many changes to the surface of the planet. The fundamental patterns of bedrock geology, erosion, and vegetation, however, present a basically unchanged backdrop against which we can view the distribution of cultural features. Applying this principle to the study of aerial photos means that examination will proceed from small-scale to large-scale imagery (Fig. 5.10). In a regional study conducted to locate archaeological sites, analysis starts with a two-dimensional examination of the region. Landforms, drainage patterns, erosional characteristics, and vegetation zones are outlined and used to infer the characteristics of the bedrock and soils of the region. Once the regional structure has been clarified, the local environment is examined stereoscopically on large-scale imagery (e.g., 1:20,000 or 1:15,000). Details of the general patterning are scrutinized for anomalies that might constitute cultural features.

Analysis of aerial photos may lead to the formation of hypotheses about the potential of a given landscape or habitat to support human occupation at various levels of technolgy. For example, in a study of the east coast of Hudson Bay, Harp (1974) first sought to determine the region's potential for human habitation. From the patterns of vegetation and fauna he deduced that a coastal sea-mammal-hunting orientation was the only viable subsistence strategy for hunter-gatherers of the region. This deduction led to examination of large-scale photos of coastal inlets that could provide both good hunting areas and favorable locations for settlement. The photos showed a number of anomalous features which, upon ground survey, proved to be the remains of prehistoric houses clustered in settlements. Further ground survey disclosed sites not directly detected on the photos.

At this point, it is useful to discuss what to look for when examining aerial photos for traces of human habitation. Traditionally, three kinds of *signatures* are basic to archaeological analysis: shadow, soil, and crop marks. Shadow marks reveal slight elevational differences that might go unnoticed by a ground observer. For example, the ridges and furrows of a prehistoric agricultural field may have been almost completely obliterated by erosion or later land use. Photographed at the right time of day, however, the linear light-and-dark patterns resulting from slight shadows may stand out clearly on a photo. The highly eroded remains of sites and structures may also show up as shadow patterns on aerial photos.

Quite a different kind of signature is the soil mark. Human use of a place results in the addition of foreign organic and rock materials to the soil. It also affects the compactness of the soil and the arrangement of existing sediments. To the extent that these changes have an effect on the reflectivity of the soil when viewed from the air, the outline of a settlement, of certain parts of it, and foundations of structures present within it are seen as soil marks.

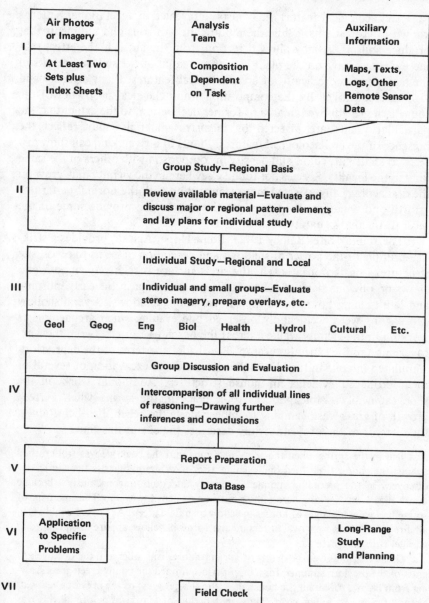

Figure 5.10. Air photo analysis. The diagram shows the major steps in the analysis of environmental and cultural features of a landscape using aerial photographs. (Adapted by permission of The University of New Mexico Press from an article by Jack Rinker in *Photography in Archaeological Research*, editor Elmer Harp, 1975.)

Archaeological features may also be revealed in vegetational patterns known as crop marks. While the modification of soils and sediments that produce soil marks may allow detection from the air, it is the effect that these changes have on the plant growth potential of the soil that results in the most sensitive indicator of archaeological features. Plant diversity and vigor are controlled by the compositional and chemical properties of the soil. Plant growth over an area of former occupation, to the extent that the particular plants are affected by intrusive materials, may reflect the presence of the archaeological features. Plants of a given kind can show differences in height, color, and density in comparison with others of the same kind in the locality. Species not found elsewhere in the vicinity may grow on the archaeologically affected area. Contrasting with the normal pattern of growth and zonation, crop or vegetation marks can provide some of the most distinctive signatures.

The Ipiutak Site (Rainey 1971), Point Hope, Alaska, provides a striking example of the power of shadows and vegetation patterns to reveal site structure. Located on a beach, the site's surface is relatively smooth and shows no obvious signs of subsurface features except in the early morning and late evening hours when the sun casts long shadows. Several shallow depressions were accidentally observed one evening when archaeologists working in the vicinity walked across the beach en route between their excavations and the expedition camp. The shadow patterns of the depressions stimulated interest in the Ipiutak locality, and test excavation of several of them produced evidence of house structures. Additional work on the topographically visible patterns took place in the spring when a fresh growth of grass was beginning to appear along the beach. Froelich Rainey, the director of the project, vividly describes the site at this time.

. . . late in the spring when the snow had gone and the pack ice was still crushed against the shore, I returned one evening after bird hunting across the site of our discovery of the preceding summer. Suddenly and quite unconsciously I became aware that I was walking across the site of an ancient town. . . . That moment of spring had painted a map of houses in yellow on a field green. As far as I could see in all directions, there were oval or rectangular forms in yellow, apparently arranged in parallel rows like streets.

Grass growing over the debris of ancient houses was taller and the dead yellow grass of the previous summer, for a brief period, topped the young green grass growing from below. All about the house sites, the shorter grass of the previous year was already topped by a new crop. Thus, in a period of ten days, before all this was equalized, working very long days indeed, I was able to measure and draw a map of 575 houses. (Rainey 1971:7.)

Although these observations were made on the ground, they illustrate the potential of this kind of evidence. Clearly, the observation and recording of these signatures would be enhanced in aerial photographs of the site.

With this general discussion of aerial photography in mind, we can turn to some examples of its application. The studies summarized below show how aerial photography may be used for site location and outline the limitations of this application. They show also how internal site structure can be detected and how this information can provide a basis for other kinds of investigation. Several of the cases illustrate the important differences in results depending on the kind of film used and the season of year the imagery was obtained.

A study by Gumerman and Neely (1972) in the Tehuacan Valley, Mexico, illustrates the potential of false-color imagery for cultural feature identification and eco-zone demarcation in arid lands. The Tehuacan Valley was selected as a test area for false-color because extensive aerial coverage was available, the valley had an extensive record of archaeological sites and features, its microenvironments had been mapped, and one of the photo analysts had not seen the valley on the ground. Out of a group of photo series available from the National Aeronautics and Space Agency (NASA), false-color infrared (FCIR) photos were chosen because this medium had proved valuable in archaeological studies of arid lands elsewhere in the Americas. The series selected was the product of a low-altitude flight (5000 feet) over the valley. Laboratory inspection of the photos was limited to a fraction of the valley and to platform mounds and canals since the area was too large and the sites too numerous for a complete ground coverage or a complete identification of all suspected cultural signatures. Archaeologists spent one month in the field searching for physical evidence of the sites and the features identified on the photos.

The results of the Tehuacan study are summarized for several microenvironments in Table 5.3. From the figures given, it is evident that archaeological feature visibility, even in an arid zone, is controlled by the vegetational characteristics of individual microenvironments. Accuracy of photo identification was highest for travertine slopes, a microenvironment with little or no soil, and consequently a vegetation area highly sensitive to anomalous features. Cultural feature identification was poorest in the alluvial slope microenvironment. The cactus, small-leaf shrubs and trees of this zone form a forestlike canopy one to 2 meters (6.5 feet) above the ground and effectively screen or blur any vegetational or soil marks that might be present. Intermediate success was had in the alluvial valley center and terrace subarea. In this area, mounds were visible because farmers avoid them in cultivation. The three sites known to be present in the area, but not identified on the photos, were sherd scatters with no raised structural ruins. The overall conclusion of this study was that FCIR imagery was unsuited for cultural feature identification in thorn thicket forests and that for the other zones the signatures probably would be equally clear in panchromatic photos.

Table 5.3. A Test of False-Color Infrared Aerial Photography for Archaeological Site Discovery in the Tehuacan Valley, Mexico

	Alluvial Valley Center and Terraces	Travertine Slopes	Alluvial Slopes (Thorn Forest)
Total items	20	11	11
Percent visible	85%	100%	0
Percent not visible	15%	0	100%
Number correct	17	10	0
Number incorrect	0	1	0

An index of the success of discerning archaeological sites and features located within 3 ecological subareas of the Tehuacán Valley through the study of false-color infrared photographs. *Total items:* the number of sites inspected on foot in each of the ecological subareas. *Percent visible:* the percentage of sites and features visible on the photographs within each individual ecological subarea. *Percent not visible:* the percentage of sites and features not visible on the photographs that were present within each of the ecological subareas. *Number correct:* those sites or features which are visible on the photographs that were correctly identified as to their function. *Number incorrect:* those sites or features which are visible on the photographs that were not correctly identified as to their function. From *American Antiquity* 37(4):520-27.

On the Gulf Coast of Mexico, in the state of Veracruz, Bruder and associates (1975) used aerial photos to locate sites at the mouth of the Papaloapan River (Fig. 5.11). The jungle vegetation of this area contrasts sharply with the semidesert conditions of the Tehuacan Valley. Working with normal color and FCIR imagery acquired from flights at 450 meters (1500 feet), the archaeologists examined clearings in the mangrove forest for photographic signatures of potential archaeological significance. They found that light-colored flecks or rings, and dark clumps or rings, within the clearings were highly accurate predictors of site location. Field examination showed the sites in most cases to be approximately 10 meters (32.5 feet) in diameter and 20 centimeters (8 inches) to 2 meters (6.5 feet) high. In one part of the study area, 58 of 61 identifications were confirmed on the ground.

In addition to their use for site location, aerial photographs can also elucidate details of site layout. An early example of aerial photography from the eastern United States illustrates this type of usage. In this case, vertical airphotos were taken of an obliterated section of the Newark Earthworks, a central Ohio Hopewellian ceremonial center constructed and used between A.D. 400 and 500. The modern community of Newark, founded in 1801, had destroyed most of the site, although portions of it have been preserved or restored. Most of the site was mapped in the 1840s (Squier and

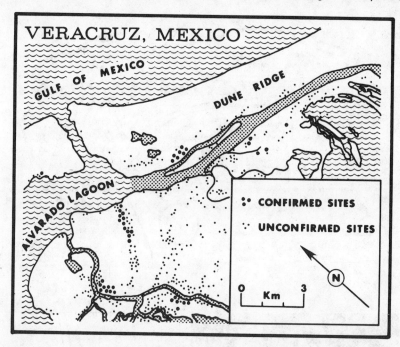

Figure 5.11. Archaeological sites in the Lower Papaloapan River, Mexico. Inspection of aerial photographs led to the identification of potential archaeological sites. A field check was conducted to determine which of the aerial "signatures" actually represented a site. (Adapted from Bruder et al. 1975)

Davis 1848), but a part of it described as an avenue formed by two low, parallel ridges extending for 2.5 miles (4 kilometers) from the main earthworks area was not included on the published map (Fig. 5.12).

In the winter of 1934, Captain Dache M. Reeves photographed the Newark Earthworks from an elevation of 3077 meters (10,000 feet) (Reeves 1936). Clearly visible on the photographs were two parallel lines representing streaks of light-colored soil. These soil marks could not be explained by cultivation patterns, current or abandoned roads, or any other recent land modification. When the photo was matched with the early map, however, it was clear that Reeves had found the unmapped causeway.

An unanticipated result of this pioneering experiment (Deuel 1969:222) was the discovery of a portion of the earthwork that not only had not been mapped in the original survey but also was not mentioned in field notes or publications. Near the terminus of the main causeway, Reeves observed a short branching corridor, closed off by a circle, and the possible evidence of

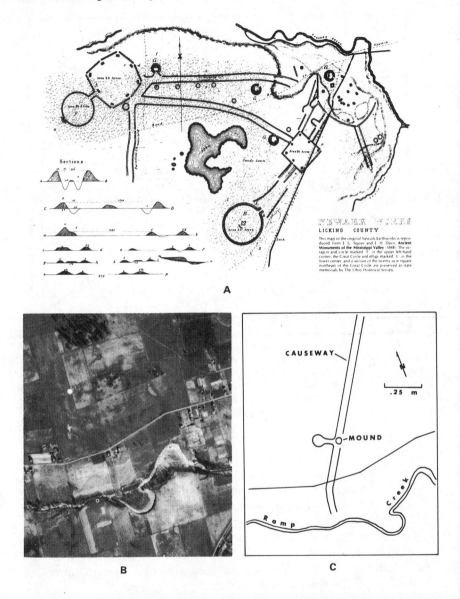

Figure 5.12. Aerial photography of the Newark Earthworks, Ohio. (A) A map of the site made in the 1840s. (B) An aerial photo of an unmapped portion of the site. (C) Line drawing of the additional site features observed on the aerial photo. (Reproduced from Reeves 1936 by permission of The Smithsonian Institution.)

a leveled, circular burial mound where this branch met the main causeway. Therefore, in addition to confirming the extension of the mapped corridor, the aerial photography contributed new information about the site.

Another example of determining site layout from aerial photography is given in the experimental work of Hampton (1975). Four sites in England consisting of multicomponent occupation from Neolithic through Roman occupation periods were photographed at five different times of the year (June 4, June 19, July 7, July 30, and August 15) to monitor seasonal variability. The work was a test of the value of multispectral photography as well as of seasonal differences in exposure. Photographic series for panchromatic film with a blue filter, panchromatic with a yellow filter, normal color film, and false-color infrared were obtained on each flight.

The diagram in Figure 5.13 shows that different film-filter combinations produce a more complete picture than any one combination alone.

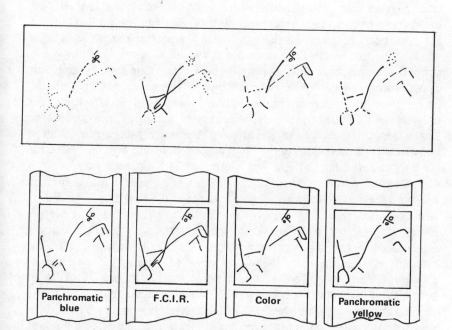

Figure 5.13. Aerial photography of the Willesley Warren Site, England. Analysis of crop marks on the photos disclosed a network of ditches and embankments. The illustration shows a portion of the site and the differences in detail and image quality recorded by four simultaneously exposed frames. (Adapted by permission of The University of New Mexico Press from an article by J. N. Hampton in *Photography in Archaeological Research*, editor Elmer Harp, 1975.)

Different aspects of the complex pattern of house foundations, fences, and other structural remains were brought out by each emulsion. Panchromatic with blue filter was the least effective of the four combinations. Normal color was found to be effective mainly in the early stages of research, as a measure of crop condition. Panchromatic film with a yellow filter together with FCIR produced the best interlocking and complementary coverage, taking account of seasonal variability and inherent color spectrum differences.

In addition to site survey and site layout mapping, aerial photography can be used to organize the surface collection or excavation of a site. This is illustrated in the University of Washington examination of the Caples Site (45-SA-5) on the Columbia River, near the Bonneville Dam, in southwestern Washington (Dunnell et al. 1976). The purpose of the project was to determine for the Corps of Engineers whether any part of this site contained undisturbed deposits worthy of preservation. A portion of the site with the circular depressions of 35 housepit dwellings had been excavated in the 1930s, but no report was issued. Amateur collectors had dug uncontrolled holes in the same portion. Since the site was within the planning area for enlargement of the Bonneville Dam reservoir, it was necessary to find out if any cultural remains were left that could be further damaged by reservoir development. It was evident that the housepits themselves had been almost totally destroyed, but space between houses was potentially intact, and the existence of an undisturbed occupational zone south of the housepit area was suggested by surface-exposed artifacts. Because digging and cultivation had obscured the locations of the housepits, and because no map existed for the site, an aerial photo flight was contracted with a private firm.

An FCIR photograph of the Caples Site was acquired during a flight in May at a scale of 1:3600. Although not taken at the best time for moisture stress on plant growth to show the maximum diversification in vegetation marks, the photo reveals several distinct patterns with potential cultural significance (Fig. 5.14). Most importantly, the area known to contain the housepit depressions displayed a number of round and rectangular signatures, deep red in color and, in some cases, outlined by bluish or brownish tones. For excavation purposes, the rectangular and round signatures were distinguished as separate sampling strata. Two other signatures—mottled colors between the circles and rectangles, and a large blue area—were considered as a single stratum in the sampling plan. The photo signatures, therefore, were interpreted as a reflection of functional diversity in the structure of the site. This hypothesis served as the basis for a randomized sampling plan which directed attention to various parts of the area. On completing the excavation, although it was apparent that the

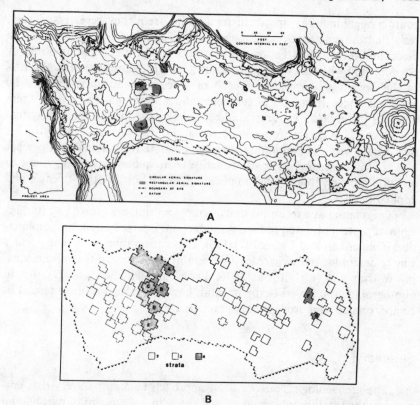

Figure 5.14. Aerial photo interpretation of the Caples Site, Washington. (A) Topographic base map of site showing potential cultural features (circular and rectangular "signatures") and the site boundary. (B) Sampling divisions ("strata") based on interpretation of the aerial photography. (From "Remote sensing in archaeological sampling designs," by Robert C. Dunnell, Figures 4 and 5. *Transportation Engineering Journal* 106:349-363. 1980.)

signatures in many cases had been misinterpreted, archaeologists pieced together a basic outline of occupational history and internal patterning. The site was found to have been occupied intermittently or seasonally between the late thirteenth and sixteenth centuries A.D. Furthermore, although containing little evidence of housepit dwellings, the southern half of the site was found to contain an occupation zone unmodified except by the action of plowing.

Aerial photography is but one of a number of data-collecting systems within the broad field of remote sensing. Also included are scintillation counters, gamma ray spectrometers, radio frequency receivers, lasers, radar, and magnetometers, among others. These instruments are used to detect and record information on the nature and properties of an object or phenomenon without coming into contact with the subject matter. Normally, the devices are carried in aircraft or spacecraft and thus separated by great distances from the phenomena under investigation. All of them measure phenomena in forms undetectable by the human sensory system (e.g., force fields, electromagnetic radiation, and acoustic energy). This fact, along with the panoramic coverage possible from a distance, is what makes remote sensing such an attractive technique in archaeology, not to mention geology, forestry, urban planning, and a host of other sciences and applied fields.

Originating as a technical study, remote sensing has grown to a full, integrated system of data production, reduction, interpretation, and explanation (Gumerman and Lyons 1971:126). Experimentation is currently under way to determine the archaeological usefulness of many of the various sensing instruments (e.g., Lyons 1976; Lyons and Hitchcock 1977). Aerial photography, though still experimental, has had enough positive results to be appreciated as a proven tool in archaeology.

Summary

The archaeological survey is an approach to data recovery that emphasizes the location, observation, and recording of remains of past human activity that are visible or detectable on the earth's surface. All survey work is regional in scale and aims to render a broad picture of the archaeological remains in an area. The information obtained by a survey may form the initial step in a program that calls for excavation, or it can serve as data in its own right.

Survey work is performed according to the standards outlined in Chapter 4. Regions are partitioned in a grid system, or some other form of horizontal control. Units of the grid are examined methodically, the findings recorded precisely on maps, observations recorded in notebooks, and collections made, if necessary. Inspection procedures vary from project to project, but usually crew members traverse the survey units in an orderly fashion, maintaining a prescribed distance from person to person.

The probability that archaeological remains will be discovered on a survey is a function of at least five general factors: abundance, clustering, visibility, obtrusiveness, and accessibility. Rare sites or artifacts are less likely to be found than abundant ones. Clustered phenomena have a lower discovery probability than dispersed phenomena. Artifact size, composition, heat, color, and many other physical, chemical, biological factors are important in the obtrusiveness of artifacts. Site area and artifact size and density are among the factors that determine the visibility of sites and artifacts. Finally, the ability of the archaeologist to reach the location of archaeological remains has a strong influence on the discovery probability of those phenomena. These factors must be taken into account when one plans an archaeological survey and they must be accounted for in the analysis. Steps can be taken to overcome the impediments to discovery, but it must always be remembered that because of these factors, the archaeological record is never seen in its totality, or seen exactly the same way from season to season.

Information about sites located on a survey is recorded on a special site survey form. These forms differ from project to project, but several categories of information are common to all. Sites are numbered according to one of several standard systems and the location determined in reference to one or several map coordinate systems. Previous investigations are noted and land ownership is registered. The form also includes data on the natural setting of the site and its dimensions, structure, relation to other sites, and estimated age and cultural phase. In order for subsequent form users to understand the conditions of discovery, notes are added about survey method. Additionally, references to other sources of information on the site are given. Of critical importance is a note on the condition of the site and a recommendation for future investigation. Finally, no site form would be complete without a map of the site.

Upon discovery, or at a later phase of investigation, sites often are investigated intensively by one or several techniques. Controlled collections of surface-exposed artifacts are often very revealing about the overall structure of a site. Soil characteristics also preserve site structure and can be used to advantage with the right techniques. Electrical resistivity and thermo-remanent magnetism are two basic forms of geophysical prospecting that involve mapping of subsurface features. The information obtained from these various approaches can be used to organize the structure of an excavation, or it can be used on its own merits to solve a problem.

Most surveys emphasize the location and recording of dense concentrations of artifacts, or sites. Therefore, they disclose data for the solution of problems related to the organizational and developmental characteristics of human groups in settlements. They do not produce data on the direct relation of human groups to their environment. Because of this shortcoming, an approach called the nonsite survey has emerged. The nonsite survey emphasizes, in its most rigorous form, the location and recording of individual artifacts rather than clusters of artifacts. Survey units are located to sample the environmental diversity of a region, and all space is examined with equal intensity. With exact or small grid unit locations on artifacts, sites can be defined at desired density levels, and questions of settlement patterns can be addressed as successfully as questions of land use. In an extreme variation of the nonsite survey, no exact locations are recorded, but instead artifacts are collected within large units. The important quality of a nonsite survey, therefore, is not the form of artifact recording, but rather the commitment to equal examination of all relevant forms of environmental variation. This approach to survey is seen by some as essential to the successful pursuit of questions of changes in subsistence levels.

One of the most important and rapidly growing fields of remote-sensing investigation is aerial photography. A bird's-eye perspective has intrinsic advantages over a ground view, and aerial photography has therefore always been attractive to archaeology. Its appeal has grown with the increased emphasis and interest in regional problems and increasing sophistication in photography and airborne vehicles. The photographic possibilities are as varied as the means of getting a camera in the air. Whatever the medium of photography or camera vehicle, the basic interpretive concepts are routine. The process of examining aerial photos for archaeological information begins with a study of the large-scale natural features and narrows down to these features which can be ascribed only to cultural activity. By and large, the remains of human activity are detectable as crop marks, shadows, or soil marks. The ground identification of certain of these signatures with archaeological features permits an interpreter to map cultural distributions from the photos and cover a large amount of territory on a tabletop in a short period of time. Although in many respects in its infancy, the archaeological interpretation of aerial photography promises to be one of the most valuable tools of archaeological research in years to come.

In conclusion, archaeological survey is a many-faceted aspect of archaeological data recovery. Since the surface is more accessible than the subsurface, it is natural to look first at it for an appraisal of the archaeological resources of a region. The information gained from the surface can be used to make reasoned decisions about how to pursue the more elusive subsurface information. Or, it can be used as a source of primary data. The latter usage is gaining ground as regional problems attract more interest, and as evidence accumulates that surface-exposed data are not as seriously disturbed or distorted as formerly believed. While still mostly a means of locating sites with excavation potential and solving simple distributional problems, the archaeological survey is gaining in importance as a way of producing primary data for the solution of major problems of cultural growth and change.

Chapter 6

Excavation

Most research problems call for the kinds of information that can be revealed by excavation. When a site survey indicates that enough plant and animal remains exist to disclose dietary patterns and subsistence ecology, and the general distribution pattern of artifacts promises a viable reconstruction of past community organization, then excavation is undertaken to test the hypotheses derived from survey information. Knowledge about environment and climate during occupation is also sought through excavation.

Essentially excavation strategy is based on a distinction between the vertical and horizontal dimensions of an archaeological site. The distinction is important because of the interpretive difference inherent in the two dimensions (Wheeler 1956). The horizontal dimension preserves contemporary relationships between artifacts; it permits reconstruction of the daily life of a community. The vertical dimension preserves temporal relationships from which stages in the development of a settlement can be traced. A project focused exclusively on sociocultural reconstruction will be designed to remove strata one by one, while a culture-historical project will focus on cutting through layers. These fundamental approaches may be portrayed as mutually exclusive, but in actuality they are to some degree integrated in any given project.

To discover whether the kinds of data required by a research design are present in a site, and in order to decide on which general approach to adopt in full-scale excavation, archaeologists must test a deposit. This chapter begins with a consideration of the ways test data can be produced. The test data provide information on the general vertical and horizontal structure of a site, and its contents. With this background, an excavation strategy can be planned in detail.

While in a sense every excavation is a unique application of the general principles discussed in Chapter 4, a number of standard approaches have evolved over the years. Some of the more common ones are described following the section on testing. The excavation of features and burials is performed in much the same way as general site excavation, but a separate section is devoted to this topic to identify some methods and techniques specifically that pertain to small-scale excavation problems.

No discussion of excavation would be complete without mention of the tools employed in excavation, and their respective tasks. Screens are becoming more and more common on archaeological digs and a complete section is devoted to some of the pros and cons of screening. A section follows on the collection of samples for ecological, geological, and dating purposes. The chapter concludes with some comments on the kinds of records typically maintained to document the progress of an excavation, the structure of the site, and the artifacts and samples observed and collected.

Testing

Excavation cannot begin until a general image of the horizontal and vertical structure of a site is known. One way to obtain this picture is to apply one or several of the methods of intensive surface examination discussed in the previous chapter. Another approach is to test the subsurface deposit with various probing devices, or to dig small test pits or trenches. From both sources of information a preliminary conclusion can be drawn about the number of temporal and functional components represented in the site, the kinds and quantities of artifacts present, and the nature and complexity of the stratification. Such intelligence is absolutely necessary for the effective placement of full-scale excavation units.

The testing of subsurface deposits can be done by probing with solid rods, by removing cores of dirt, and by manual or machine excavation of pits and trenches. The test type chosen for a given project, the number of tests to be made, and the location of test spots naturally depends on the research problem under investigation. Although it is undertaken as a preliminary to full-scale excavation, testing does require adherence to the standards of archaeological method. Therefore, notes must be maintained on the procedures and the results of the testing, and the locations of all tests must be recorded on a map.

The scheduling and extent of test examination of a site depends upon the total program of research. Some testing may be done at the time of discovery of a site. In that case, usually the intention is to determine whether the site has a subsurface manifestation in good condition. A test will also determine the nature of stratification and of the artifacts present at the site. These initial tests may consist of one or two hand-dug pits. The pits may be informative about the vertical structure of the site, but they do not reveal variation in stratigraphy for the entire site, nor do they provide much information about horizontal variation in the distribution of artifacts. As an excavation planning tool, therefore, testing must be more extensive. Because extensive testing is time-consuming and labor-intensive, it usually is done in a separate phase of investigation.

Probing. One of the simplest testing instruments is the rod probe used by drainage tile contractors to locate old tile lines. A pointed steel rod with a handle at one end is pushed perpendicularly into the ground. Differences in the amount of resistance can be sensed as the rod penetrates through various strata. A general idea of the site's stratification can be obtained in this way.

Shovel testing. Shovel testing can be used to determine site perimeters in cases where vegetation reduces visibility to near zero. Chartkoff (1978) has described the use of shovel testing to obtain this information. Working with hunting-gathering campsites, two in Michigan and one in Italy, Chartkoff dug shovel "potholes" at regular intervals on transects that either radiated from find spots or were offset from a base line located in relation to surface exposures. Depending on the size of the site and density of recovered artifacts, the sampling interval varied from long (10 to 20 meters) to short (3 to 5 meters). Odd-shaped holes, rather than measured squares, were dug because experimentation showed precision to be unnecessary and time-consuming. Chartkoff also points out that the more formalized, rigid, and intensive transect shovel-testing becomes, the less useful it is. At a low intensity it has the potential to determine a site's boundaries and perhaps its internal variability, with the advantages of low cost and minimal destruction to the deposit. At a high intensity, however, it can be costly and destructive. If intensive testing is needed, consideration should be given to larger test pits, excavated in a conventional manner.

Test-pitting and trenching. The most common form of testing is manual excavation of pits and trenches. In shallow sites, units one meter (3.25 feet) square are the standard; sites over a meter deep require larger sizes, and units one by 2 meters (3 by 6 feet) are often used. To be maximally effective, test pits should be excavated slowly. In fact, they probably should be done with greater care than the full-scale excavation since the findings of the test pits will be used to design the full-scale attack. It is important to learn as much as possible about the site's sediments and soil development during the testing stage. The design of an excavation plan depends on the ability to identify strata, which in many cases may be subtly different in composition and color, and extremely thin.

Test pits and trenches may produce samples of artifacts and other archaeological material, and may completely or partially expose features. In a general sense, therefore, information on the kinds and quantities of artifacts and features present in the site is obtained. This information probably is most reliable for estimating vertical change. If the testing intensity is 5 to 10 percent of the site area, it may also permit estimation of the horizontal structure of a site. Especially for the lower strata, this knowledge can be critical in the design of full-scale excavation.

Power equipment. In some cases, power-driven equipment is used to test a site. One of the most frequently used machines is the backhoe, which consists of a bucket-shaped scoop mounted on the back of a tractor or similar vehicle and operated hydraulically to dig a trench. On floodplains, backhoes have been used as a means of site discovery when it is known that most sites of a particular period are deeply buried and seldom seen on the surface (Chapman 1977). In such cases, and more typically when a site location is known, the machine-dug trench walls are scraped clean and straightened vertically by hand. This allows study of the deposit's stratification. Because of the rough action of backhoes little control is maintained over artifact recovery. Therefore, artifacts are sacrificed for stratification; this is one reason the backhoe is used predominantly on endangered sites that must be salvaged quickly or lost completely.

Post-hole testing. Post-hole diggers, both manual and power-driven, with diameters of approximately 15 centimeters (6 inches), have been used in testing. These implements are highly destructive and do not retrieve columns of dirt, as in coring, but they can be of value where a large area requires immediate and speedy attention. An example from Mesoamerica illustrates the benefits of manual post-hole diggers.

As part of the Tikal Sustaining Area project, the purpose of which was to examine the region surrounding the monumental ceremonial district of the Classic Period Mayan site of Tikal, Robert Fry (1972) experimented with the use of post-hole diggers to determine where to locate controlled test pits around house mounds. The Mayans erected their houses on low earthen platforms known as house mounds to raise them above the level of flooding. Information on the dates of construction and occupation was an important aim of the Sustaining Area project. Because Mayan ceramics are often highly decorated and have provided precise chronologies for the entire region, dumps around the house mounds containing potsherds would offer an important source of data.

In the rain forest environment of Tikal, jungle vegetation obscured the surface around the mounds, and the location of the major part of a dump was rarely evident. Apparently all such mounds had dumps, but their locations varied from the sides of the mound to the back. The front, which faced a court, or plaza, generally was free of refuse. To reduce the number of unproductive test pits, Fry had his crews dig post-hole tests around the mounds to locate the densest, deepest layer of the trash. The procedure entailed the random selection of mound groups for testing, post-holing around the sides and backs of the mounds in the selected group, and formal test-pitting after location of productive areas. The post holes were dug down to sterile dirt or to bedrock and the number of sherds in each hole was recorded. Test pits were located next to the most productive post holes. In this manner the problem of low visibility was overcome by use of an extremely common tool to hasten accomplishment of the project.

Core testing. A coring device removes a plug or column of dirt so that soil variation can be directly observed. Manual coring tubes range from about 2 to 10 centimeters (¾ to 4 inches) in diameter and can penetrate several meters below the surface. Power-driven models mounted on vehicles can produce core tests as deep as 76 meters (250 feet). Coring cannot yield an artifact sample as may be obtained through manual test-pitting, but it can be done with great speed. Therefore, a large number of test cores can be obtained and a comprehensive picture of a site's stratification reconstructed in a relatively short time. The following examples of deep coring with power-driven equipment illustrate the importance of this type of testing.

The first example is from preliminary work at the St. Albans Site, on the bank of the Kanawa River in West Virginia (Price et al. 1964). In 1963, after overburden was removed from the floodplain to provide fill for highway construction, an amateur collector in the region observed artifacts on the surface and in a cutbank exposure. Of particular note were projectile points of a type dated elsewhere in the region to about 5000 B.C. These points suggested that the site might contain a stratified sequence of the area's Archaic cultures.

Later in 1963, a power-driven coring device was brought to the site in order to determine its potential for intensive excavation. The specific objective was to determine the horizontal extent of the deposit, the degree of construction disturbance, the depth of the deposit, and its stratification. Using a pipe 8 centimeters (3 inches) in diameter, removed from the drill hone in one-meter (3-foot) intervals, a total of six cores were taken. The first was located near the cutbank where evidence of occupation was visible. After that, cores were located in a grid pattern perpendicular and parallel to the bank (see Fig. 6.1). The deepest core penetrated 11.2 meters (36.5 feet) below surface.

As a result of the coring, it was possible to delimit the boundaries of the site on the basis of charcoal content. Charcoal density in each level

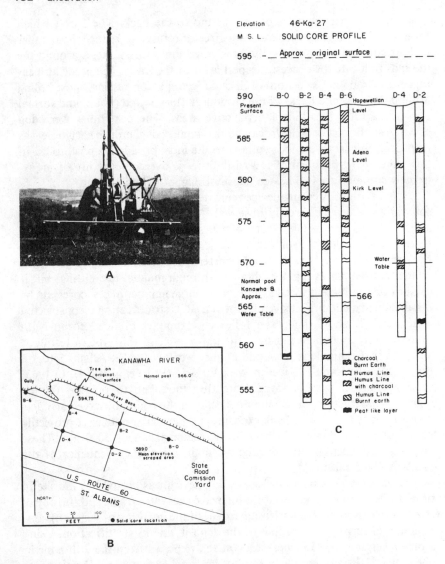

Figure 6.1. Core drilling at the St. Albans Site, West Virginia. (A) Core drill rig in operation. (B) Site map showing core locations. (C) Solid core profiles. (Reproduced from Price et al. 1964 by permission of The Society for American Archaeology from *American Antiquity* (30(2):219-222.)

decreased in all directions away from the first hole. Layering was difficult to discern precisely, but at least 15 strata were visible in the core columns. It was clear, also, that the site contained abundant artifacts and that it was deeper than suspected from the evidence of the cutbank. Subsequent to the coring, an excavation program emphasizing horizontal exposure of the successive occupation layers was planned and carried out over a period of four years (Broyles 1971).

A second instance of core drilling occurred in Monks Mound, located in Illinois on the Mississippi River across from St. Louis. This mound is the largest prehistoric structure of its kind in North America and probably the largest earthen structure in the New World. A terraced structure 31 meters (100 feet) high with steep, sloping sides and a flat top, the mound covers 7.2 hectares (18 acres) at its base and is estimated to contain approximately 616,000 cubic meters (22,000,000 cubic feet) of earth. It was built in stages between A.D. 900 and 1150 by sedentary agricultural peoples of the Mississippian cultural tradition. Along with smaller mounds, Monks Mound formed the center of Cahokia, a prehistoric metropolis estimated to have held 30,000 people at the peak of its occupation (Fowler 1974).

In 1965 and 1966, drill holes were sunk in seven places on the top of Monks Mound (Fig. 6.2) and at two locations on its terraces. Cores of earth were obtained by driving steel tubes that measured 60 centimeters (2 feet) long and 8 centimeters (3 inches) in diameter into the ground with a truck-mounted hydraulic ram. The cores from each drilling were pieced together to form a complete column for each hole drilled. The purpose of the work was "to obtain a broad and general understanding of the history of the mound in the form of hypotheses which would facilitate future intensive excavation, as well as fill in the gaps in our knowledge of the Cahokia settlement" (Reed, Bennett, and Porter 1968:138).

From the base to the top of the mound, a distance of 31 meters (100 feet), 14 distinct levels were located (Fig. 6.2B). Each level is thought by the excavators to represent a constructional stage in the mound's growth. Each level consisted of a limonite soil band which might have been produced by oxidation of an exposed surface. Excavated Mississippian mounds elsewhere in the eastern United States show evidence that the surfaces of structures were burned at periodic intervals, and the mound surfaces were raised with the addition of each new structure. The limonite bands perhaps represent similar events at Monks Mound. It is estimated that rebuilding took place in 18-year intervals. This is the probable life span of the mud-walled, thatched-roof structures which undoubtedly served as temples, worship places, priest residences, or administrative buildings during the 250-year span of the mound's history. Thus a credible hypothesis about the

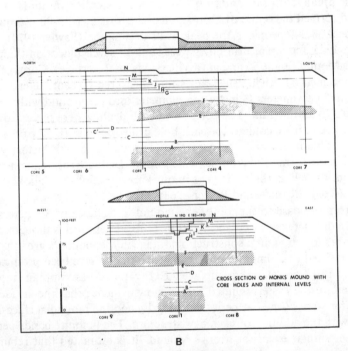

Figure 6.2. Core drilling at Monks Mound, Illinois. (A) Aerial view of the mound. (B) Interpretation of the core profiles showing major internal soil features. (Reproduced from Reed et al. 1968 by permission of The Society for American Archaeology from *American Antiquity* 33(2):137-148.)

mound's internal structure was derived from the core testing and can serve as a guide in the excavation of this massive prehistoric construction.

The extent and kind of testing will depend on the research problem. Culture-historical research, for example, may not require extensive testing, except to determine that a site is stratified. Problems in the domain of sociocultural reconstruction require broad horizontal exposures and are more likely than culture-historical problems to involve extensive tests.

Some Standard Approaches

Over the years a number of standard approaches to excavation have evolved (see Fig. 6.3). They differ in the manner of progression through a deposit and according to the type of site being excavated. Whether they are designed primarily to obtain a vertical or horizontal exposure, or to permit both views is another variable. The following descriptions are organized in terms of the latter factor.

Trenching. The most effective way to obtain information on the vertical structure of a site is to trench it. The continuous profile exposed on a trench wall is invaluable for the structuring of a large-scale horizontal excavation, and it can provide the basic information needed for a culture-historical problem. Trenches vary considerably in length, but generally do not exceed 5 meters (16 feet) in width. The wider the trench, the less suited it is to provide the kind of data for which it was designed. Trenches most often are seen in parallel series (Fig. 6.3A) or crisscrossed at right angles (Fig. 6.3B).

The removal of dirt from a trench can be accomplished in many ways, but one common approach is *step trenching*. By this approach, trenches are excavated from one end to the other, and individual strata or levels are exposed in step fashion before being excavated for the entire length of the trench. This is done because of the need to collect samples and record observations by strata. The perception of strata in a trench is often difficult, and step trenching brings the strata into relief and physically outlines them so that they may be more effectively removed. The procedure is usually seen in trench excavations of sites and features whose margins are steep slopes (e.g., platform mounds and village tells), or which have been cut through by erosion.

Vertical face method. The vertical face approach involves the excavation of adjacent trenches from one end of a site to the other, recording features and artifacts as they are encountered. The exposed face of a trench is profiled before advancing to the next trench. The method is best suited

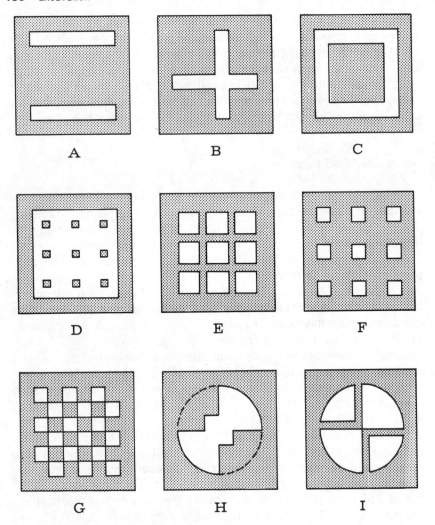

Figure 6.3. Basic excavation layouts. (A) Parallel trenches. (B) Intersecting trenches. (C) Isolated block. (D) Post method. (E) Squares and balks. (F) Isolated squares. (G) Alternate squares. (H) Hourglass quadrant. (I) Staggered balk quadrant.

for the excavation of artificially constructed mounds with uncomplicated and clearly delineated stratification and has been applied with success to burial mounds and to substructure mounds. It also has been used to excavate mounded shell middens in the eastern United States. The results have been poor in the latter case, however, since shell mound strata consist of innumerable thin shell lenses, and correlation of the profiles from one cut to another is difficult.

An obvious limitation of this technique in general is that it provides profiles along only one grid axis. The intersecting profile is not observed directly and cannot be drawn except by extrapolation from points on the existing profiles. This may be acceptable in cases of simple stratigraphy; complex sites, however, cannot tolerate a great deal of assumption in the reconstruction of their layering. This drawback can be overcome in a number of ways. At Hiwassee Island in Tennessee, Lewis and Kneberg (1946) were able to preserve one intersecting profile by retaining a balk through the center of a mound, perpendicular to the trenches (Fig. 6.4).

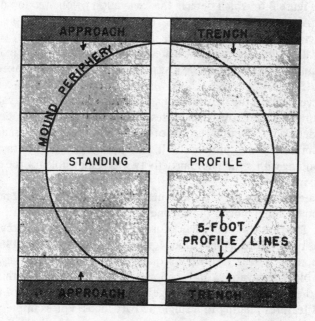

Figure 6.4. Burial mound excavation plan. (From Lewis and Kneberg 1946)

The vertical face approach does not completely ignore the horizontal dimension. In fact, as noted above, it has been applied chiefly to burial mounds in which the objective of excavation has been not only to observe and record the succession of layers, but also to expose the graves covered by the mound. Excavation of the Nowlin Mound in Indiana (Black 1936) illustrates this facet of the approach (Fig. 6.5). This Adena cultural tradition burial mound measured 52 by 22 meters (170 by 70 feet) at its base and was 4.6 meters (15 feet) high before excavation. Gridded along its long axis, the mound was sliced like a loaf of bread in 1.5-meter (5-foot) cuts from end to end. Burial tombs encountered during the slicing were left in place as the excavation proceeded, thus producing a horizontal exposure of the most prominent features of the mound.

Isolated block approach. Another standard approach which combines vertical and horizontal exposures is the isolated block approach. By this method, trenches are dug around an area that is subsequently excavated by a method of horizontal exposure, such as level stripping (described below). This approach provides an excellent view of the strata and thereby overcomes the difficulty of observing strata changes, a problem experienced when working from the top of a deposit. An example of this strategy is shown in Figure 6.6, which depicts the excavation of one section of a shell mound in Alabama (Webb and De Jarnette 1942). In this example, following the excavation of two parallel trenches through the midden, two additional parallel trenches were excavated perpendicular to the first two to form a standing block of the deposit. The block was then staked out in 1.5-meter (5-foot) squares, each of which was excavated in 15-centimeter (6-inch) levels within the natural units. The purpose of this excavation was to learn how the numerous shell lenses of the mound had been deposited. With the detailed horizontal records of this block, the complex sequence of shell accumulation was unraveled. It was possible to determine to what degree flooding rather than human activity was responsible for the observed stratification.

Block excavation. Excavation methods with an exclusively horizontal orientation include block, plow zone stripping, and level stripping approaches. The first two approaches form a key part in the research strategy suggested by Binford (1964) and formalized by Struever (1968). This strategy consists of the following sequence of operations: survey, test excavation, block excavation, and stripping. Block excavation in this context refers to the excavation of units large enough to contain within them the items and features relating to a single activity locus. For example, butchering, cooking, tool preparation and repair, and recreation are activities that frequently coexist in space. To the extent that it is possible to locate activity

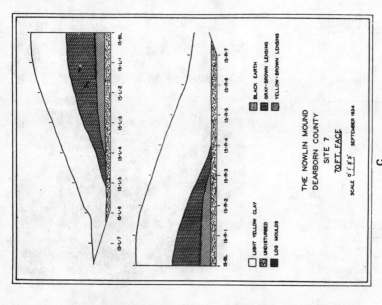

THE NOWLIN MOUND
DEARBORN COUNTY
SITE 7
70 FT. FACE

SCALE 0 1 2 3'   SEPTEMBER 1934

C

A

B

Figure 6.5. Vertical face excavation of the Nowlin Mound, Indiana. (A) General view of excavation. (B) The 70-foot face with burial tombs in foreground. (C) Profile drawing of the 70-foot face. (From Black 1936)

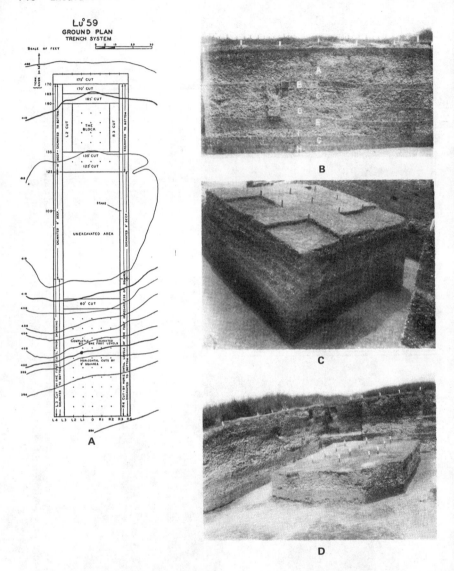

Figure 6.6. Isolated block excavation of Site Lu° 59. Alabama. (A) Ground plan of the excavation showing the isolated block in the upper portion of the map. (B) Profile of one side of the block, on the 160-foot grid line, showing natural strata. (C) The block at the beginning of excavation. (D) The block at completion of the excavation. (From Webb and De Jarnette 1942)

loci such as these through surface collection and other techniques of intensive surface investigation, the units of continuous exposure in excavation can be oriented to them.

Block excavation is best adapted to small sites with well-preserved occupation floors as are typical, for example, in Archaic Period sites in the eastern United States. On large sites, unless it is possible to achieve almost total excavation, the use of blocks risks the danger of learning too much about too little of the site. Time and money are wasted if the details of one or two activity loci are recovered without corresponding information on the total structure of the site. Block excavation may also be counterproductive on sites which do not show evidence of well-preserved occupation floors. The seasonal flooding of eastern United States Archaic campsites often seals each successive occupation in clay. In arid lands, however, such conditions do not occur as commonly. The typical floodplain deposit is a soft, sandy silt in which artifacts and other occupation debris are easily displaced up and down from their original position. The disruptive effects of pedestrian activity by the original residents, rodent activity, and the freeze-thaw cycle make the occurrence of intact occupation floors in such soils a rarity. The successive floors common in floodplain sites in the eastern United States are inextricably blended together in the arid west. Block excavation can recover the pattern of dispersion, but not the individual occupation floors.

When blocks are excavated in stratified deposits, steps must be taken to preserve a visual record of the strata within the block. One way to do this without sacrificing the broad horizontal exposure of the block is to retain square pillars or posts of dirt at the intersecting grid lines (Fig. 6.3D). This is not a completely satisfactory answer to the problem, for as the excavation deepens, the posts become higher and more precarious. Another tactic is to excavate squares within the block at different rates and to draw profiles before proceeding to adjacent squares, as in the isolated block approach described above.

Plow zone stripping. On shallow sites, block excavation can be followed by stripping, unless the blocks cover the entire area of occupation. Stripping is done most commonly with power equipment, such as road graders, and involves removing the upper portion of the deposit which has been disturbed by plowing to expose archaeological features. Immediately after being cleared, the stripped surface is troweled by hand to smooth it out and facilitate inspection of it for features. Features located by this process are mapped and their contents carefully excavated by hand and saved for analysis. Some features may have been already exposed and mapped in the block excavation phase. When these features are combined with those disclosed by stripping, a picture of the entire community, and of community growth in time and space, can be documented.

Level stripping. A method for the horizontal examination of the individual units making up a stratified mound is called *level stripping*. As applied (Fig. 6.7) to the excavation of a Mississippian Period (A.D. 600 to 1650) temple mound in Tennessee (Lewis and Kneberg 1934), it involves two stages. In the first stage, test trenches are excavated into the mound from the cardinal directions. The purpose of the trenching is to locate the surfaces of the individual strata. Therefore, when a stratum surface is encountered, downward excavation ceases. If the first surface is deep in the deposit, the trench is continued vertically until other surfaces, originating closer to the center of the mound, are found. If a surface is found high in the mound, it is cleared completely before workers go to the lower layers. Basically, the trenching conforms to the step trenching approach. In the second stage of level stripping, the surfaces are excavated in their entirety to expose traces of the structures where they once stood.

The Wheeler-Kenyon method. A common combination of vertical and horizontal approaches is referred to as the Wheeler-Kenyon method (Wright 1969), named after the British archaeologists who pioneered in the amalgamation of the stratigraphic and "architectural" methods. Dever (1973) termed the combination the *balk/debris-layer method* and outlined some of its advantages and pitfalls. By this approach, vertical control is maintained through the use of balks or ridges to separate digging areas (Fig. 6.8). Excavation within grid squares emphasizes the complete excavation of a debris-layer, or stratum, over the entire excavation before proceeding to the next lower layer.

A *balk* is a wall of dirt between two adjacent pits, both of which have been excavated (Fig. 6.3E). Balks vary in thickness and may be as narrow as 20 centimeters (8 inches) or thick enough to provide a raised walkway through an excavation. The squares in an excavation using balks commonly are 2 to 5 meters (6 to 16 feet) on a side. At a minimum, they must be large enough for a worker to move around in comfortably. The maximum size of a square depends on the size of the site, the size of the features normally encountered in the site, and the depth to which the excavation is being taken. In excavations over 2 meters (6 feet) deep, large units are employed so that as the unit deepens its area can be reduced in a step fashion. This lessens the danger of wall collapse and enables workers to get in and out.

Four problems normally are encountered in the application of the balk/debris-layer method. First, it requires detailed work and thus is limited to small exposures, which on large sites may seriously impair exposure of the overall layout. Second, the balks are barriers to visual perception of the

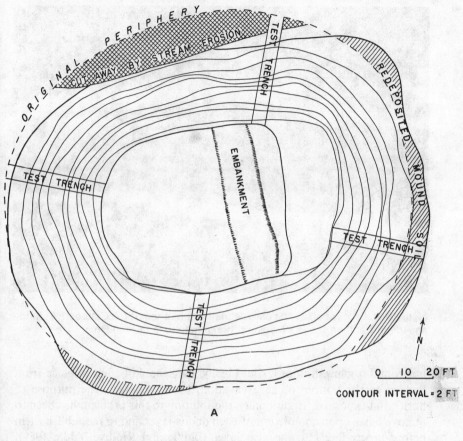

ORIGINAL PERIPHERY

CUT AWAY BY STREAM EROSION

REDEPOSITED MOUND SOIL

TEST TRENCH

TEST TRENCH

TEST TRENCH

EMBANKMENT

TEST TRENCH

N

0   10   20 FT

CONTOUR INTERVAL = 2 FT

A

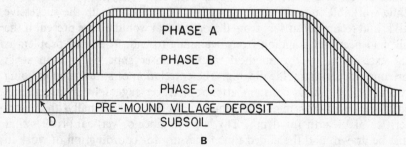

PHASE A

PHASE B

PHASE C

PRE-MOUND VILLAGE DEPOSIT

D

SUBSOIL

B

Figure 6.7. The strategy of level stripping for the excavation of Temple Mounds at Hiwassee Island, Tennessee. (A) Contour map of Mound 37 showing location of coordinate test trenches. (B) Diagram of excavation strategy. (From Lewis and Kneberg 1946)

Figure 6.8. Excavation by the balk/debris-layer method of the Galbreath Mound, an Adena tradition (Early Woodland) burial mound in central Ohio.

horizontal organization of a site. Ideally, they should be left in place from the top to the bottom of an excavation, but this defeats the purpose of horizontal exposure. Traditionally, the solution to this problem has been to remove balks upon completion of each debris-layer and to reestablish them before proceeding into the next layer (Biddle and Kjolbye-Biddle 1969). While workable in theory, it is actually difficult to link up the successive balks, and recording suffers from distortion that would not be present if the balk had been left standing from beginning to end. The third problem is that excavation by this method requires closer supervision than strict horizontal or stratigraphic digging. The correlation of strata is an ongoing process that demands constant attention. Dever suggests that in extreme cases one supervisor might be required for each pit. Finally, there is a sacrifice of breadth for depth. The large number of vertical profiles that must be drawn, and the added time necessary for coordination of work in individual pits, inevitably results in a compromise between allocation of time to expansion of horizontal coverage and increasing the depth of excavation. Dever thinks that horizontal coverage will suffer. These problems do not, however, make the system unworkable. As in any actual field situation, careful thought must be given to the problem of which sites, or which parts of a single site, require this approach.

Isolated pits. Excavations at the Early Neolithic (about 7000 B.C.) site of Jarmo, Iraq, illustrate an attempt to use a large number of isolated pits to obtain information on community plan (Braidwood and Howe 1960). Step trenching and level stripping in the 1948 and 1950 to 1951 seasons had established the site's stratigraphy and exposed a portion of the village at various periods in its history. The work of the first two seasons had opened approximately 6 percent of the total village area, estimated on the basis of surface exposures to occupy 1.3 hectares (3.2 acres). It was decided that knowledge of the total village plan would be a valuable supplement to the stratigraphic and structural information obtained in the first seasons. However, at the rate of excavation achieved in the first seasons, it was estimated that total excavation of the site, layer by layer, would require a crew of 50 excavators for 25 seasons.

The time constraints of this estimate suggested that a short cut was necessary, and it was decided that a systematic pattern of "test pits" 2 meters (6 feet) square and separated by 4 meters (13 feet) would be excavated rather than large exposures. Arranged in the pattern shown in Figure 6.9, 151 pits were dug, averaging 1.75 meters (6 feet) in depth. The test-pitting, which increased the sample to 11 percent, was not a success, however. The excavators report that

unfortunately, what this test-pit system showed us most clearly is that there are no short cuts for examining what goes on underground. The intermittent sections have still to be studied in detail, but it appears that the extrapolation of completely meaningful sections which we had hoped for will be impossible. The underlying strata of archaeological sites may pitch and toss in ways which their present surface contours seldom suggest; the conventional lecture-hall analogy of archaeologists that the layers in a mound are like the layers of a cake is a vast oversimplification. In Jarmo, the pitching and tossing seemed to be excessive in some portions of the mound. (Braidwood and Howe 1960:39.)

Thus, it would appear that this approach is not satisfactory for horizontal exposure unless done at a sampling percentage higher than 10 percent.

Although not entirely successful in the Jarmo case, the isolated pit approach deserves serious attention. At sampling levels of 20 percent or higher, the approach is potentially more productive than others in producing information on overall site structure. Currently block excavation is the favored method of obtaining information on site structure. In choosing it, however, a sacrifice is made. Since it involves the opening of large areas of contiguous squares, block excavation is expensive in time and labor; other large areas of a site must be excluded. The result is that a great deal is

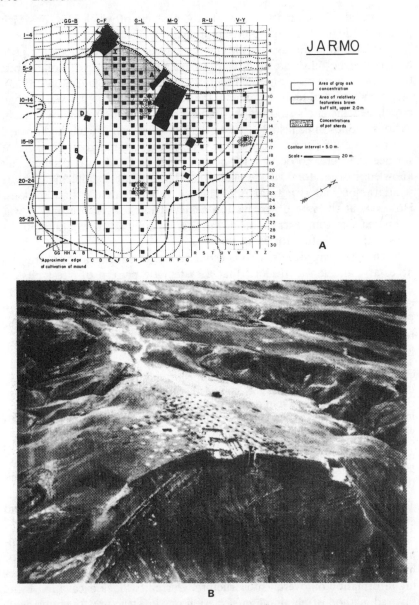

A

B

Figure 6.9. Isolated pit excavation of Jarmo, Iraq. (A) Location of excavation units: the isolated pits are shown as solid squares oriented at right angles to the grid system; units A and II were excavated by step trenching. (B) Aerial photograph of the site. (Reprinted from "Prehistoric Investigations in Iraqui Kurdistan," *Studies in Ancient Oriental Civilization*, Braidwood and Howe, by permission of The University of Chicago Press. ©1960 by The University of Chicago.

known about certain areas, and nothing about others. It is entirely conceivable that at the end of a project that emphasizes block excavation, information about the total structure of the site will not have been obtained. Therefore, the isolated pit approach may be seen as a viable alternative, or as a first stage followed by block excavation after site structure has been defined. Isolated pits may be the exclusive approach to sites in which occupation floors are not present, a condition which obtains commonly in hunting-gathering sites in arid regions.

Alternate squares. Another example of an approach that attempts to obtain vertical and horizontal exposures simultaneously is the alternate square method. The excavation of alternate squares gives maximum horizontal dispersion for a 50 percent sample and at the same time produces uninterrupted stratigraphic exposures along all grid lines. This approach was applied with success by Sanger (1970) in the excavation of housepit depressions at the Lochnore Creek Site, British Columbia, Canada. Figure 6.10 shows the excavation at a stage when the alternate square approach was in progress. Excavation began with a trench that extended the length of the site (50 meters, or 163 feet) and which was excavated in alternate 1-by-2-meter (3-by-6-foot) units. The trenching suggested that, of the four housepits at the site, Housepit 2 had been least disturbed by relic collectors. In order to get a maximal picture of the horizontal and vertical structure of the housepit, a grid with a 2-meter (6-foot) interval was expanded on both sides of the exploratory trench and alternate squares selected for excavation. Each of these units was excavated to gravel in 25-centimeter (10-inch) arbitrary levels and the profiles drawn. With the site's structure known, the remaining squares were level stripped by natural units.

The quadrant method. The excavation of burial mounds has been approached by a method commonly referred to as the quadrant, or quartering, method. After deciding on the way that a vertical profile is to be preserved (either by staggered balks or by the walls of adjacent, unexcavated quadrants), archaeologists proceed with excavation by level stripping. Burials and other features are exposed as in the vertical face method and enough of the mound is dug to permit complete exposure and recovery of the interments. Since the center location is often the preferred place of burial, the excavation need only include opposite quarters and the center of the mound to produce the hourglass layout in Figure 6.3H. Equally often, however, burial placement and general mound structure are more complicated, and nearly complete excavation is required. In such cases staggered balks are used for stratigraphic control (Fig. 6.3I). Excavation can be carried to the point that the balks are removed once they have been profiled, photographed, and drawn.

Excavation of the Cresap Mound in West Virginia (Dragoo 1963) illustrates an application of the quadrant approach (Fig. 6.11). The mound,

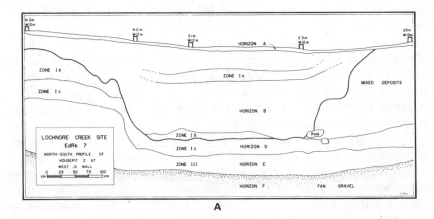

A

B

Figure 6.10. Alternate square excavation at the Lochnore Creek Site, British Columbia. (A) Stratigraphic profile of Housepit 2. (B) Excavation pattern at Housepit 2. (Reproduced from Sanger 1970 by permission of The British Columbia Provincial Museum.)

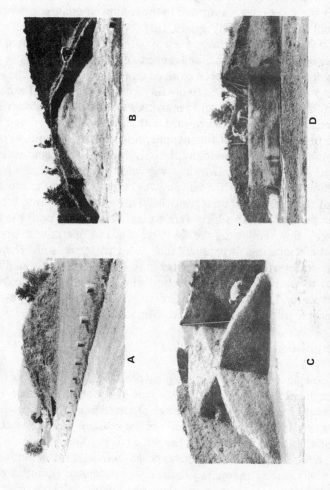

Figure 6.11. Quadrant excavation of the Cresap Mound, West Virginia. (A) The mound before excavation. (B) Southwest quadrant after removal of uppermost stratum. (C) Profile walls of the inner mound. (D) Excavation of the central block. See Figure 4.6 for stratigraphic profile and ground plan of the mound. (Reproduced from Dragoo 1963 by permission of The Carnegie Museum of Natural History.)

which measured 4.6 meters (15 feet) high and 21.5 meters (70 feet) in diameter before excavation, contained the skeletal remains of individuals of the Adena cultural tradition. The general findings of the excavation are described in Chapter 4. The first step in the Cresap excavation was to dig a trench 3 meters (10 feet) wide and 15 meters (50 feet) long on the western edge of the mound. This operation exposed a small portion of the mound and displayed its contact with the natural soil profile. On completion of the trench excavation, the crew was moved to the southwest quadrant. Working in units about 3 meters (10 feet) square, they level stripped the quadrant to the top of an inner mound surface which apparently had been exposed long enough after being erected for a humus zone to develop in it. Balks one foot (30 centimeters) wide that had been retained along the grid lines of the excavation were profiled and removed to obtain a complete horizontal exposure of this stratum. After drawing and removing burials on the surface of the inner mound, they excavated downward within the grid squares, again retaining one-foot balks. Except for the innermost square, all units were excavated to the bottom of the mound, burials and features being sketched and removed upon discovery. Drawings were also made of the balks before they were removed so that when bottom was reached all but the square at the center of the mound had been removed. This square was left to provide support for the axial balks which were to be left standing until the final stage of excavation. Following the same sequence of operations, workers excavated the remaining three quadrants down to sterile soil. Then the block at the center of the mound was taken to the bottom and, finally, the axial balks, to obtain a complete vertical and horizontal picture of the mound's structure. Excavation of the Cresap Mound shows how excavation within a general framework is adjusted to specific characteristics.

Excavation of Features and Burials

Archaeological features, such as pits, post molds, house floors, and debris concentrations, along with burials, are common elements of an archaeological site. Features such as storage or cache pits often contain artifacts, tools, ornaments, and plant and animal remains in better states of preservation than found generally in the rest of a site. The material in them was buried from the start and was not exposed to the destructive influences of daily activity during the period the site was occupied. Burials are particularly important in this respect, for they were intentionally constructed to provide a protected resting place for an indiviudal or group of individuals, and the things buried with them. Another significant quality of features and burials is that they represent or include items that can be assumed to be in contemporaneous and behavioral association. The things scattered at random throughout a site, although close to one another and forming meaningful distributional patterns, seldom have accumulated at the same time. Features, on the other hand, are composed of materials that are coeval, items that must have come together at the same time in order for the feature to have been formed in the first place, and to be archaeologically recognizable later. One more important aspect of features and burials is that they are building blocks in the reconstruction of a settlement layout. Patterns only hinted at in the general distribution of debris acquire a more cohesive explanation when the remains of firepits, houses, and the like are added to the picture.

The approaches to feature and burial excavation are those applied to a site as a whole, on a smaller scale. Since features and burials cannot be recovered as a whole, but rather are destroyed as they are uncovered, they must be taken apart carefully. Each step of the way must be documented by notes, sketches, maps, and photographs.

Three basic strategies exist for the excavation of features and burials. In the *pedestalling* approach, items are left in place on columns of dirt so that the horizontal and vertical arrangement of things can be seen and documented. This approach is most useful for material that is scattered on a surface, such as an occupation level or the floor of an abandoned house or room. Another expedient is to dig out the fill of a feature, plotting the locations of internal items in cases in which important relationships are represented. Fill removal is particularly valuable in burial excavation and in the excavation of cache pits, storage pits, and post molds. It works best when the outlines of the feature are clear and easy to follow. In combination with pedestalling and fill removal, features and burials can be *sectioned*. In this approach, the feature is cut vertically along the major axes, at least, in order to obtain a visual record of the contours of the feature. Fill is removed and internal items are plotted as the excavation advances.

Thomas (1975) described the sectioning approach as it was applied to the excavation of 114 Late Woodland refuse pits with stratified fill in the Fort Hill Site in New Hampshire. After the surface dimensions of the pits had been mapped, one quarter of the feature was selected for excavation on the basis of its orientation to sunlight. (A sunlight orientation is desirable at this stage because the excavator must be able to view the pit outline clearly in vertical section.) Small tools, such as trowels or spoons, were used to remove dirt by strata. The dirt was screened to recover material missed in the initial digging and to obtain small samples of faunal and floral refuse. Upon completing this quarter, workers profiled the walls and evaluated the stratigraphy. In this stage it is often difficult to perceive layers in the detail seen on a vertical cut when digging down through a feature (or any deposit, for that matter). When the strata had been identified clearly, the remaining three quarters were excavated in turn. Detailed information was thus obtained on the internal contours of the features, as viewed along the two axes, and data were gathered on the accumulation of refuse within the pit. This type of information is used in the correlation of refuse types with types of pits, and in studies of change in diet through the years as revealed in the successive layers of refuse.

In any feature that consists of a large number of discrete items, especially in the case of burials, it is best to work from the center outward. This reduces the danger of displacement of, or accidental damage to, individual items. When excavating burials, field workers must take care not to damage the surface of the bones. Some archaeologists recommend the use of blunt tools made of a soft material for burial excavation.

Excavation Tools

The kinds of tools employed in excavation are as varied as the problems of archaeology. And because the scale and requisite precision range from massive removal of culturally sterile overburden to minute examination of features, the size of excavation tools varies greatly as well, from bulldozers to teaspoons and needle-sized probes. Despite the diversity of tool size and function there are a number of tools that are common to most excavations.

Routine digging requires a shovel, pick, trowel, whisk broom, dustpan, and some form of container for dirt removal. In most excavations, shovels are the major dirt-moving tool. Both round- and square-nosed types are good to have on hand, but the number of each will depend on the soil. Round shovels work best in clay soils while square ones are most appropriate for sandy soils.

Picks of various sizes are useful where particularly hard sediments are encountered. In arid environments, for example, calcium is carried downward by soil moisture and forms a cementlike layer when it dries. This layer is impenetrable by shovel and must be attacked by pick. Picks are quite destructive even when skillfully wielded, but extreme situations call for extreme means! Generally speaking, large, heavy picks cannot be controlled well enough to merit a prominent place in the excavation tool kit. Smaller varieties that have a hoelike blade opposite the pick are quite useful, however. Pick-mattocks, as these implements are called, are lightweight and thus easily manipulated: soil is loosened with the pick and then crumbled with the mattock.

The star of an archaeological tool kit everywhere is the trowel. The kind of trowel best suited to archaeological work is the mason's pointing trowel. Originally designed to smooth and inscribe cement mortar, this trowel adapts well to the scraping and probing functions of archaeology. Edge sharpened and beveled, the blade is held obliquely against the floor of a pit and drawn toward the excavator. Dirt is removed in thin, crumbling slices so hardly a thing escapes notice. The pit floor is maintained in a smooth condition that is essential for detection of the outlines of features. The point of the trowel can be used to make shallow probes if buried items are suspected in an area of the pit.

In shallow sites less than one meter (3 feet) thick and in sites that contain numerous features, trowels may be used exclusively. Small sites with detailed stratigraphy may also require the exclusive use of trowels and other small tools. More commonly, however, shoveling is the primary means of excavation, and trowels and other small tools are brought into play only upon encountering an item of significance, or to excavate features and burials.

Indispensible companions of the trowel are the whisk broom and the dustpan. The working floor of an excavation should be kept clean at all times in order that features may be seen and the progress of work measured. To accomplish this, workers can move dirt scraped up during troweling directly into a dustpan for removal from the pit. Periodical brushing with a whisk broom, or a large paint brush, goes even further toward maintaining a clean floor. If this sounds like housework, the point is well made, for the process and the reasoning are exactly parallel to keeping house.

An archaeological tool kit contains a number of other small items that are handy for the excavation of features. Dental picks, narrow paint brushes, root clippers, kitchen paring knives, grapefruit knives, and other instruments are in demand at one time or another on a dig. Burial excavation, in particular, requires a wide variety of delicate tools.

Discarded dirt ultimately is dumped in a backdirt pile. Wheelbarrows or buckets and baskets, alone or in combination, are used to transport dirt from pit to dump. Quite often, dirt is passed through a screen before it reaches the dump to collect small items overlooked in shovel and trowel examination. No matter how efficient or representative hand sorting procedures may be, screening usually produces a larger sample of smaller items. Balanced against time and project objectives, a screen can provide a standardized procedure for comparative purposes.

Another important supply item on a dig is a set of containers for storing recovered artifacts. Paper bags of various sizes are often used because of their low cost, but cloth bags are preferred for their greater durability. Plastic, glass, and metal containers are particularly useful for soil, charcoal, pollen, and other small environmental samples.

Recording artifact locations is a distinct operation that requires a unique set of tools. Basic in the recording tool kit are the tape measure and the level. The most useful tape is a 2- or 3-meter, rolled, pocket variety. The carpenter's line level that can be suspended from a taut string is commonly used in vertical measurements. Some situations, such as burials, demand more precise instruments, but most recording can be handled with these two items. Additionally, simple drafting supplies such as a clipboard, a drawing board, straight-edge, protractor, and compass are needed, along with pencils, paper, erasers, masking tape, and other supplies.

To Screen or Not to Screen

Although shoveling and troweling when done slowly and conscientiously are quite successful in the recovery of small items, and rapid shoveling by skilled excavators, though missing some small items, produces a representative sample of the larger items, the careful screening of excavated dirt has become more and more frequent in recent years. The increased use of this technique can be attributed in large part to the rising interest in "ecological" or "environmental" archaeology. Information on plant and animal remains is important in understanding culture-environmental articulation. Since these materials are usually small, unobtrusive, and often poorly preserved, traditional troweling and shoveling usually do not provide adequate samples. Screening is also employed to obtain large, representative samples of materials like potsherds and lithic debitage. The question of whether to screen or not is controversial. It is instructive to examine some experimental comparisons of screening and excavation with hand tools.

Meighan (1950) provides some exact figures on the difference in efficiency and accuracy between shoveling and screening. A test of the two techniques was performed during excavation of a California shell midden (the Estero Mound, 4-Mrn-232) on Drake's Bay, Marin County, California. Excavators were instructed to locate and record artifacts *in situ* by shoveling. After removal from a pit, however, excavated dirt was passed through a 1.5-centimeter (0.5-inch) mesh screen, poured down a chute to the beach below the site, and screened a second time after being washed. Of a total of 375 items recovered, 283 (75 percent) were found during the shovel removal

Table 6.1. Comparison of Shoveling and Screening Artifact Recovery at the Estero Site, California

Artifact Types	Items Recovered by Shoveling		Items Recovered in Screen after Shoveling		Total Items Recovered	
	N	%	N	%	N	%
Bone beads	6	2	4	4	10	3
Porcelain fragments	14	5	7	8	21	6
Projectile points*	47	17	22	25	69	19
Charmstones*	9	3	4	4	13	3
Bone tools*	25	9	10	11	35	9
Cut bird bones	12	4	2	2	14	4
Flake scrapers	35	12	13	14	48	13
Sinkers*	7	2	2	2	9	2
Iron spikes	2	1	3	3	5	1
Pestle fragments	15	5	4	4	19	5
Mortar fragments	30	11	7	8	37	10
Stone core tools	56	20	5	5	61	16
Miscellaneous tools	25	9	9	10	34	9
Total	283	100%	92	100%	375	100%

Adapted from "Observations on the Efficiency of Shovel Archaeology," by Clement W. Meighan, Table 1, in *Reports of the University of California Archaeological Survey*, no. 7, pp. 15-21. 1950.

*Includes fragmentary specimens.

of dirt and 92 (25 percent) in the screens. Only 2 of the screened items came from the beach operation.

The distribution of 4-Mrn-232 items by artifact type, as shown in Table 6.1, illustrates several differences between shoveling and screening. The artifact types are arranged from the top to the bottom of the table in order of increasing size. An expected result of this test case is that small items are underrepresented and large items overrepresented in the shovel sample. For example bone beads represent 2 percent of the total shovel sample and 4 percent of the screen sample; conversely, the larger stone core tools represent 20 percent of the shovel sample but only 5 percent of the screen sample. This is because large items are easier to observe during shoveling than small items. It is interesting, however, to compare the percentages of artifact types recovered by shoveling with those for the total sample (shoveling plus screening). For seven artifact types the percentages are the same; there is a difference of 1 percent for four types, of 2 percent for one type, and of 4 percent for one type. While such differences are important in the analysis of a given class of artifacts and in statistical comparisons of sites, they are negligible when the assemblage is considered as a whole and do not significantly affect conclusions that might be drawn from a shovel sample regarding kinds and frequencies of activities the assemblage represents. This test case, therefore, seems to support shoveling as a technique of artifact recovery. Screening does not necessarily produce a more representative sample than shoveling.

The question of whether or not to screen has received attention more recently in connection with increasing demands for samples of small materials and for quantitative analyses of all materials. The question has been directly addressed by several British researchers. Barker (1975) has reported the results of an experiment in animal bone recovery from a small Late Neolithic to Early Bronze Age site (Monte Covolo) in Italy. Comparing the recovery of trowel excavation and froth flotation (discussed in a later section) or water screening in 0.3-centimeter (0.1-inch) mesh screens, he found that of 20,000 animal bone fragments, most of the identifiable fragments were recovered by troweling. Screening increased the number, and produced evidence of small mammals, but the proportions of caprines, cattle, and pigs were practically the same by both methods. Cherry (1975) has reported on a similar experiment at the Late Bronze Age site of Phylakopi on the Greek island of Melos. After excavating with small hand picks, field workers passed dirt through 0.25-centimeter (0.1-inch) mesh dry screens and processed it by flotation. The flotation residue water was screened. Cherry found that 65 percent of the total weight of the recovered sherds came from excavation and that the screening process, as would be expected, added smaller sherds to the sample. Examining sherds possessing definitive attributes of shape, function, or surface modification, he found that 80 percent came from excavation and that the screened material did not change the proportionate representation of the various attribute classes.

It appears that there is no single dictum to follow in deciding whether to screen or not. The decision depends on a number of factors, including the scale of the operation, the time available for its completion, the locational precision desired or necessary, the nature and size of the material, the information sought from this material, the rarity of the items sought, and budgetary considerations. Large excavations cannot, except in rare instances, screen everything, so a balance must be struck. Thus, only a fraction of the excavated ground might be screened as a check on the excavated sample and to allow quantitative comparisons. Projects of a salvage nature, or with a short-term field schedule, may not be able to afford the luxury of screening and may have to abandon it altogether, or elect to screen only a fraction of the excavated dirt. On the other hand, screening may be substituted completely, on small sites, for hand excavation. The precise location of items by shovel, trowel, or hand pick is slow work, and if precise locations are not required, the tedious hand techniques might be abandoned. If the sediments do pass easily through a screen, it may be most economical to employ screens exclusively.

The nature and size of the material in a site are also important factors in deciding whether or not to screen. If items are small, numerous, and similar in color to the soil matrix, screening may be absolutely necessary. This is particularly important for chipping debitage and potsherds. On the other hand, the small items of a given material may provide little or no information beyond that obtainable from the larger items that are easily recovered by hand excavation. So, the answer depends in large measure on the value of the small items to the research question. Also significant is the relative rarity of the items or information being sought. If tools, ornaments, or some other class of remains are known to be rare, but are essential to the goals of the project, screening is a necessary technique of data recovery.

Collection of Samples

From beginning to end of an excavation, samples of the deposit are collected for study in the field or after completion of the work. All components of a site contain clues to the occupational history of a site. Midden and specimen samples, including shell, bone, and plant remains, hold important information on nutrition, diet, population size, and season of occupation. Soil samples can be analyzed to determine the nature of the environment and of landforming processes. Samples of charcoal and other organic materials can be used to date the occupation. Pollen samples are an important source of information on environment, and in some situations, such as within storage rooms, permit inference of the types of plants that were collected or cultivated for food. Since most of these materials provide data for study of culture-environmental relationships, they are referred to as ecological samples. A list of different types of ecological samples with comments on collection technique and sample size is given in Table 6.2.

The term *midden* in general refers to the accumulated refuse in a site. More specifically, it is applied to shell heaps that formed in or near the settlements of people for whom molluscs were a staple or a prominent supplement (Meighan 1969). Midden sampling, therefore, can range from the examination of deposits largely composed of dirt to deposits of solid shell.

Table 6.2. Types of Ecological Samples

Type of Sample	Comments
Midden *	
Column	Small midden material samples taken from a column with specific dimensions.
Miscellaneous	Small midden material samples taken from a pit or trench wall, by real or arbitrary levels.
Large	Huge midden samples, taken to correct for bone bias. Weighing up to 100 pounds each, these may be taken by real or arbitrary levels.
Specimen	
Shell	Taken from real levels only. The purpose is to get whole shells of all species possible for species identification and age-ring dating. At least 15 shells per level are needed.
Bone	Taken from real levels only. The purpose is to get as many specimens as possible for species identification and possible chemical analysis.
Pocket	Taken from each naturally or culturally occurring pocket or lens requiring content identification.
Feature	Wood, stone, etc., fragments from cultural features requiring chemical analyses or special examination.
Soil	
Site	Soil from the site's real levels, taken apart from the midden samples for purposes of the standard soil chemistry tests; includes burial area soils.
Nonsite	From a nonsite pit, to determine the area's natural soil horizons and history. May be chemically examined.
Dating	
Charcoal	For dating by radiocarbon laboratories only; collected where found or desired, if amount needed is present.
Shell	For radiocarbon and oxygen-18/oxygen-16 testing; can be collected by anyone. Collect as many thick bivalve shell fragments as possible.
Pollen	Collected by a palynologist using an augur or in spot samples taken from pit walls. The specific amount needed varies and care must be taken not to contaminate the sample.
Chemical	Small vials of soil collected at intervals from a continuous vertical profile; 40-gram vials collected at 10-cm vertical intervals are sufficient.

*Midden in this list refers to shell middens.
Information from "Ecological Sampling of Midden on the in *Northwest Anthropological Research Notes* 4(2):137-52.

While the techniques of sampling differ in relation to the kind and quantity of food waste, certain general characteristics and procedures may be identified.

Column and core sampling. Midden sampling is accomplished in one of two ways. Most commonly it is done by removing a column of dirt from the side wall of an excavated unit. The dimensions of the column depend on the objectives of the project, but generally a column measures approximately 25 centimeters (10 inches) square. Columns are excavated vertically in arbitrary levels, taking care not to mix strata when stratification is present and clearly visible. In deposits such as shell middens, columns are placed so as to avoid anomalous lenses and to obtain a typical sample.

A second technique of midden sampling is coring. Although a core is generally smaller than a column, Casteel (1970) has shown that in many cases coring can provide accurate information on the proportions of material making up a midden. In a midden site near Vacaville, California, core samples 23 centimeters (9 inches) in diameter were taken in the centers of three pits, before excavation. Additional cores were taken adjacent to the column samples taken from one side wall of each excavated pit. Nearly identical results were obtained from the cores and the columns. Since coring does not require an excavation unit to be dug beforehand, and because it takes less time to obtain and to process core samples, Casteel suggests that although it does not replace full-scale excavation or column sampling, it can be used profitably to supplement and expand a normal sampling program.

Flotation and water separation. Two techniques of sample collection that have seen increasing use recently are water separation and flotation. Their use was pioneered by archaeologists who felt that the plant remains component of sites, particularly in features, was being systematically ignored by shoveling, troweling, and dry screening. Struever (1968), for example, reported that more than 90 percent of the plant materials (40,000 charred nutshells, fragments and 2000 carbonized seeds) recovered by water separation of the fill from 200 features at the Apple Creek Site in Illinois escaped detection in dry screening. Therefore, special processing is necessary to obtain a balanced picture of prehistoric diet from food waste.

Water separation is based on the difference in porosity exhibited by organic and inorganic materials and the different rates at which plant and animal remains and bones settle in water as opposed to stone. At Apple Creek, the dirt excavated from a feature was dry screened through 1.25- or 2.5-centimeter (0.5- or 0.25-inch) screens to remove large materials, such as rocks and bone. The remaining fill was then poured through a washtub, the bottom of which had been replaced with a 0.15-centimeter ($\frac{1}{15}$-inch) screen and which was suspended in water, at the edge of a stream. The plant and bone fraction was skimmed from the surface of the water with a tea strainer in the few moments that it floated before becoming waterlogged and joining the heavier rocks which had sunk instantly to the bottom of the tub. The light fraction of plant and bone fragments was subsequently subjected to a chemical flotation process to obtain separation of the plant and bone components.

In chemical flotation, the density of water is increased by the addition of a soluble salt (such as sodium chloride or zinc chloride). Carbonized plant remains and seeds float while bone sinks. Because of problems with salt encrustation and surface damage to seeds, some archaeologists prefer to use *froth flotation*. By this method, a substance known as a collector (e.g., paraffin or kerosene) is added to the solution. The collectors selectively coat particles and make them hydrophobic and aerophilic. The coated particles attach easily to rising air bubbles, and with the addition of a frothing agent (e.g., terpinol), which reduces the air-water surface tension and retards air bubble coalescence, the particles will float for some time on the surface. Advocates of froth flotation point out that it is not only less damaging than water separation, but more productive as well. For example, plant remains recovered by froth flotation from Nahal Oren in Palestine were significantly reduced in quantity when put through a simple water separation process (Jarman et al. 1972). In water separation, 62 percent of the barley remains, 58 percent of the oats, 58 percent of emmer wheat, and 28 percent of the vetches sank to the bottom.

The apparatus required for water separation and flotation vary greatly in design, and therefore in cost, but all are expensive in time and labor (Watson 1976). The decision to use one or several of them must be carefully thought out. Whenever samples of the kind produced by these methods are needed (e.g., for reconstruction of the gathering subsystem of prehistoric economy) the cost is well worth the effort.

Soil sampling. Soil samples are collected after profile drawings have been made of the stratification. Depending on the complexity of the deposit, samples are taken which will permit laboratory analysis of the sediments of each stratum. In uncomplicated deposits, only one set of samples may be needed, with others added at the discretion of the director in order to examine the same layer in several parts of the site to check for minute horizontal variation. On more complex sites, and on sites with numerous isolated excavation units, a large number of samples may be needed. In such cases, detailed analysis of particle size, coloring, mineral constituents, and chemical elements can be used to correlate the various units. The ultimate purpose of soil samples, however, is to produce information for the inference of the natural processes that formed the layers and of the envrionment of the locality at the time of occupation.

The usual procedure for collecting soil samples is to remove squares of dirt, about the same size as those taken for midden analysis, in columns that cut through the major strata of the site or excavation unit. Taking precautions to prevent contamination of a sample with dirt from another part of the profile, the worker digs out each soil sample, bags it, and marks it with a number that has reference to its provenience.

Another way to collect a soil sample is to remove an entire column, called a *soil monolith*. As described by Dummond (1963), a representative stratigraphic section is marked out on the pit wall, 15 to 20 centimeters (6 to 8 inches) wide. A hardening agent such as cellulose acetate, vinylite acetate, or liquid casein glue (Elmer's Glue) is applied in a way that the solution penetrates the soil for the length of the monolith. After the column hardens, a mounting board is placed vertically against it and the untreated soil on either side is dug away. The monolith, supported by the board, is then cut away, and a complete sample of the site's stratification is obtained. Casein glue permits a monolith 0.75 centimeter (⅜ inch) thick. Other solutions enable the removal of monoliths 1.2 to 2 centimeters (½ to ⅘ inch) thick. For analytic purposes, a monolith has an advantage over bagged samples in that the structure of the soil is preserved. A disadvantage, however, is that monoliths are bulky and therefore difficult to transport and to store. For this reason, they are seldom taken in large numbers, and when they are made, it is more as a permanent record of site stratigraphy than as a major analytical sample.

A third way of obtaining a soil sample is to remove a *sedimentary peel*. This is similar to monolith preparation since it involves the impregnation of a pit wall surface with a hardening agent and is followed by removal of the cemented segment of the profile. It differs from monolith collection because it's applied to a large area and is paper thin. Voight and Gittins (1977) describe a method, called the Lackfilm method, for producing sedimentary peels (Fig. 6.12). A pit wall is troweled smooth at an angle of 10° to 15° to prevent collapse of the peel under its own weight. The surface then is sprayed evenly with cellulose nitrate lacquer diluted with acetone and set aflame to burn off the acetone and prepare the surface for later applications. After marking off the desired portion of the prepared surface, and nailing it to prevent premature detachment, one brushes on a highly viscous lacquer/acetone solution, a section at a time. Strips of gauze about 20 centimeters (8 inches) wide then are pressed onto the surface and brushed with lacquer. After the surface has become firm and dry (generally a 30-minute wait), the margins of the film are cut with a knife and the side and bottom nails removed. The film with its adhering dirt is then peeled away from the profile either from the side or the bottom. The resulting peel can be rolled up on a dowel for transport and storage. With a record of its provenience,

Figure 6.12. The Lackfilm method of sedimentary peel production. (A) Spraying the vertical face with diluted lacquer. (B) Additional lacquer application. (C) Adding gauze reinforcement. (D) Detaching the peel after drying. (E) Detached peel showing duplication of profile features. (F) Rolling the peel for transport. (From Voight and Gittens 1977)

the peel can be used for analysis, and it can serve as a permanent record of stratification.

Charcoal sampling. Charcoal samples for radiocarbon dating require special treatment in the field if they are to produce reliable results in the laboratory. Of fundamental importance in deciding whether or not to take a charcoal sample is knowledge about the context of the observed charcoal. It must come from a primary depositional context and it must be associated with artifact concentrations, strata, or features that constitute important events in the growth of the site. Furthermore, potential sources of contamination must be searched out so that charcoal enriched through addition of recent carbon can be eliminated from consideration. The quantity of material is an additional consideration in collecting charcoal samples. Age determinations can be made with samples of one gram or even less, but most laboratories prefer larger samples than this.

In removing a charcoal sample, care should be exercised to avoid contamination through handling. Contact with the fingers is acceptable, but it is best to use metal tweezers of the spatulate kind. Smoking materials should be banned from the area and precautions taken to keep foreign material from blowing in. After being removed, the sample is placed in a metal, glass, or plastic container, or in aluminum foil and sealed in a plastic bag. Individual practices vary greatly, but in all the common factor of preventing contamination during removal and storage is paramount.

Many more materials than charcoal can be dated by the radiocarbon method. Anything with an organic component theoretically is susceptible to carbon 14 dating. Some of these materials, along with absolute dry weights, are listed in Table 6.3. As with charcoal, they must come from a primary context, have a known association with a cultural or natural event of importance, and be collected and stored with contaminant-free techniques.

Pollen sampling. Pollen is the fertilizing element of flowering plants and consists of microscopic grains that are dispersed by wind and other agencies. Pollen grains are highly resistant to biological, chemical, and mechanical alteration, and can exist for an indefinite period in the soil in a recognizable condition. The surface characteristics of pollen grains are highly distinctive, making it possible to identify plant species by examination of the spores. The science of palynology uses this characteristic to reconstruct past environments and climates. Waterlogged deposits, such as bogs and lacustrine sediments, are optimal for the preservation and accumulation of pollen, and the majority of palynological studies derive their samples from such contexts. Dry deposits also contain pollen, and thus it is often productive to collect samples from archaeological sites in order to determine the plant cover of the site locality and possibly the kinds of economic plants being brought to the site by the inhabitants.

Table 6.3. Amount of Material to be Collected for Radiocarbon Dating

Description	Dry (!) Weight		Comments
	Absolute Minimum	Desirable	
Materials generally suitable			
Wood—clean or rotten	5 gm	25-30 gm	
Charcoal	2 gm	10-20 gm	Rich, black flakes
	5-10 gm	50-100 gm	Sandy, brown
			Whole shell specimens:
Shell—carbonate	20 gm	100 gm	Hard, shiny surface
	30 gm	150-200 gm	Powdery, soft surface
Shell—conchiolin (shell protein)	500 gm	1000-2000 gm	
Grass, leaves	5 gm	35-50 gm	
Flesh, skin, hair	5 gm	45-60 gm	Fresh weight
Paper, cloth	3 gm	25-30 gm	
Peat, gyttja	30 gm	80-120 gm	Dark brown
	60 gm	150-200 gm	Light gray-brown
Bone—carbonate	300 gm	800 gm	Seldom yields a valid date
Bone—collagen (bone protein)	300 gm	800-1500 gm	Up to 10,000 years old
Bone—charred	600 gm	1500-3000 gm	Up to 36,000 years old
Materials for special projects only			
Soil—organic matter	N.A.	2-5 kgm	As research projects only
Soil—carbonate		100-500 gm	
Ceramics, plaster and mortars	?	?	Subject to research

From *Australian Archaeology,* edited by D. J. Mulvaney, p. 93 (Australian Institute of Aboriginal studies, Canberra, 1972).

The collection of pollen samples does not differ from soil sampling except that even greater care must be taken to prevent contamination. While in most palynological investigations, particularly in bogs, coring devices are used to obtain samples, in open, dry, archaeological sites, samples are obtained by removing small sections of soil in columns. A single sample is taken from each strata in the exposed wall of an archaeological unit and its provenience recorded. As with the collection of charcoal samples, considerable thought must be given to the choice of a sampling location. Sections of a profile disturbed by rodent burrowing, for example, must be avoided. Upon removal from the pit or trench wall, the sample is placed in an airtight container. It is best when the samples are collected by the palynologist who will be studying the recovered material, but in most cases the archaeologist does the collecting. The samples then are presented to the palynologist, who extracts the pollen spores from the matrix and identifies the plant species present.

Records

In addition to samples of artifacts and other specimens, an excavation results in a copious set of written and pictorial records which contain a step-by-step documentation of the excavation. No detail is too insignificant to record, unless work is retarded by excessive notetaking, so archaeological projects typically accumulate hundreds, and even thousands, of pages of notes. As much work goes into the notes as into moving dirt, since in the long run a poorly described excavation might just as well not have been done.

One type of record is the log, or journal, that is kept daily by the project director. Typical entries include notes on the objectives for the day or week, crew assignments, weather, methods and techniques, observations on outstanding finds made during the day, and interpretive ideas. Crew supervisors also maintain logs of everything that goes on during excavation and observations on the separate findings of the laborers. The laborers in some cases are required to keep notebooks, as well, although usually their observations are recorded on predetermined forms. The logs form the nucleus of the excavation records. Details of one sort or another are entered in other notebooks and on forms, but the log is the record in which all the disparate bits of information are tied together. Ideally, a basic site report can be written directly from the logs.

Another kind of record is the primary observation form. The most common is the feature form. Since, as has been pointed out elsewhere in this book, features are destroyed as they are discovered, detailed notes must be made during excavation. To ensure comparability of information from one feature to the next, standardized forms are used (an example is shown in Fig. 6.13).

Information summary forms are employed by many archaeologists to assemble observations in one place. Figure 6.14 shows a form to be prepared by a laborer or crew supervisor upon completion of an excavation unit. The capsule summary is useful for a quick review of the findings at a site. The listings of samples, photographs, and other pertinent material from the unit allows rapid location of the materials and evaluation of the extent and adequacy of documentation.

All samples are given reference numbers by type and listed on forms variously called registers, inventories, and catalogs. Aside from the identifying number and a brief description, the catalogs include provenience data, recovery date, and the names of the field personnel. This information may have been recorded also in logs or on summary forms, but it does not hurt to have it repeated. Redundancy in recording protects against loss of information if one set of records is accidentally lost or damaged. Multiple records also provide a crosscheck in case errors have been made on one set of records. Features can be cataloged in the same manner, as can almost any other record. Lists of samples and records are extremely useful in keeping track of things, and for determining at a glance how much material was recovered and recorded.

Photographs of an excavation are an indispensable part of documentation. The more photographs taken the better; many projects hire skilled photographers for the purpose. All features are photographed from different angles, at different stages of excavation, and with different films. All profiles are photographed, as are the working floors of each unit as excavation proceeds downward. Shots are taken of the crew at work, and of the entire site at various stages. Vertical photos taken from scaffolding, ladders, or balloons are of immense value in photographic documentation of an excavation. Each exposure is recorded in a notebook with information on the type of film, the camera, lens, aperture, timing, and other technical data. This information is necessary for later use of the photographs in analysis and publication. It is also useful if during the excavation it is found that films, lenses, and settings adopted at the beginning of the work are producing inadequate photographs. Studying the exposure data can remedy the situation in the future.

CHIEF JOSEPH CULTURAL RESOURCES SURVEY

SUMMARY FEATURE RECORD

Site ______________________ Ref. ______________________

Unit ______________________ Director ______________________

Feature No. ______________ Excavators ______________________

Type ______________________ Date Begun ______________________
Pit, Post, Earth Oven, etc.

Whole/Partial ______________ Date Completed ______________________

Description ____
____
____
____

Upper Depth from Surface ______ cm @ ________

Lower Depth from Surface ______ cm @ ________

Upper Width ______ cm Lower Width ________ cm

Plan Shape ________ Profile Shape ________

Associations:
Exclusive ____ Inclusive ____
Intrusive (partial) ____ Intrusive (total) ____

Contents (+/-)
__ Fire-cracked rock
__ Charcoal
__ Bone
__ Vegetal
__ Shell
__ Lithics
__ Burnt Soil
__ Surfaces

Associative Features ______________________________
Ref Nos.

Float Samples ____________/______________________
Partial / Total Ref. Nos.

Soil Samples ______________________________
Ref Nos.

Radiocarbon Samples ______________________________
Ref. Nos.

Photos ______________________________
Ref. Nos.

Comments ____
____
____
____
____
____
____
____
____
____

Recorded by ____________/______
Name Date

Checked by ____________/______
Name Date

(over)

Figure 6.13. Archaeological Feature Form.

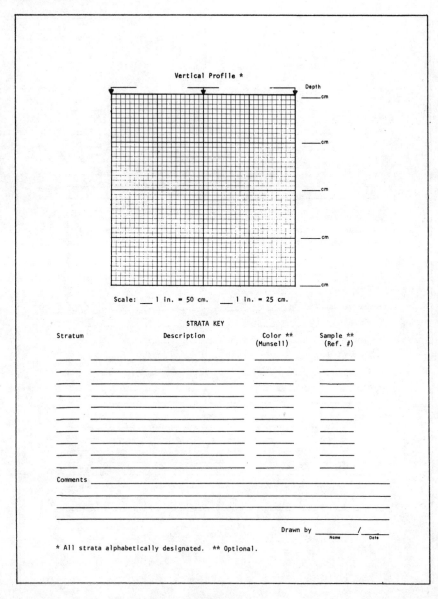

Figure 6.13—*Continued*.

Darby Dan Farm Project: EXCAVATION UNIT SUMMARY

1. Unit: _____

2. Dimensions: length _____ width _____ thickness _____ volume _____

3. Arbitrary levels: no. _____ thickness _____

4. Recovery method: _____
   _____
   _____

5. Stratification: _____
   _____

6. Features: _____
   _____

7. Exact locations: total _____ inventory nos. _____
   _____
   _____

8. Unit locations: total _____ inventory nos. _____
   _____
   _____

9. Samples: _____
   _____
   _____

10. Profiles recorded: __ N __ S __ E __ W (check if recorded)

11. Plans recorded: _____

12. Field note references: _____

13. Photographs: _____
   _____

14. Personnel: _____

15. Dates: _____ 16. Recovery time: _____

17. Manhours: _____
                                        WSD   6/76

Figure 6.14. Excavation Unit Summary Form.

Summary

Excavation is undertaken to recover information on settlement structure and on changes in artifact styles and community patterns through time. Depending on the specific research problem, excavation emphasizes either the horizontal or vertical dimensions of a site. In order to know whether a site contains information of the type required by a research problem, and in order to successfully design full-scale excavation, it is necessary to test a site. Testing can be done by probing with solid rods, coring with manual and machine-operated tubes, and digging test trenches and pits by hand or by machine. The kind and degree of testing depends on the research problem.

When the vertical and horizontal structure of a site is known through testing, an appropriate excavation strategy can be designed. For strictly vertical excavations, trenching at various intensities is the most common approach. Trenches are often excavated in steps to maintain control over stratigraphic location and ensure the accurate recording of artifacts. The vertical face method is a common way of excavating burial and other artificial mounds. By this approach, the mounds are sliced like loaves of bread. The isolated block approach provides a balance between vertical and horizontal approaches. Trenches are excavated around a grid block to trace individual strata around the entire unit. The strata preserved in the block then can be accurately removed one by one.

Excavation approaches with strictly horizontal emphasis include the block, stripping, and level stripping methods. Block excavation is designed to obtain complete exposure of the major functional districts of a site. In single component sites it is possible to strip the overburden from an occupation layer upon determining the general structure by intensive surface examination, testing, or block excavation. In stratified sites, the various levels, or strata, can be removed successively by level stripping. This approach is most commonly applied to stratified mounds.

The balk/debris-layer approach to excavation is a combination of horizontal and vertical approaches that attempts to produce an integrated picture of a site's structure. Excavations of this type are crisscrossed by standing vertical walls of dirt between excavation squares. This approach is applied most often when horizontal exposures are desired for sites with complicated stratigraphy.

The acquisition of structural information on large sites is a problem which can be solved through the use of isolated pits. Because excavation is costly in time and money, the block and balk/debris-layer approaches are often inefficient, since these approaches concentrate effort in small areas. It is more profitable to reduce excavation unit size and scatter the units out.

The alternative square method maximizes horizontal dispersion of excavation units and can produce continuous profiles along all grid lines. At intensities of less than 50 percent, the method can be used effectively to increase the amount of horizontal exposure and maintain continuous exposures in linear "transects" through a site.

Mounds often are excavated in quadrants. This approach is like slicing a pie and achieves horizontal exposure of mound contents while at the same time preserving continuous vertical profiles along the major axes of the mound.

It should be emphasized that the various approaches described are seldom used in isolation. In any given excavation one approach might be used on one part of a site and another elsewhere. Or, as in the Binford-Struever strategy, different approaches might be used at different stages of the excavation. The principle objective of excavation is to acquire desired information. The way the information is produced, or acquired, can vary greatly. The approaches described here are simply some of the more common ones.

The excavation of features and burials parallels excavation of a site as a whole. Several techniques that apply specifically to features and burial excavation are pedestalling, fill-removal, and sectioning. Because of the importance of features in preserving a contemporaneous set of artifacts, special care is taken to document the precise relationship of all elements of the feature. The same is true for burials.

The tools employed in excavation are as varied as the problems and approaches of archaeology. Tools as small as tweezers and dental picks are required in burial excavation and in the removal of charcoal samples. In the initial stages of testing, and for removal of culturally sterile overburden, mechanized equipment such as bulldozers and backhoes is often used. Intermediately, there are items used in all types of dirt moving: shovels, picks, wheelbarrows, and so on. One of the most common archaeological tools is the trowel. Borrowed from the brick-laying craft, the flat "tuck-pointing" trowel is handily adapted to scraping thin layers of dirt in archaeological work. On many projects that emphasize wide exposures and precise location of all artifacts, the trowel is the exclusive instrument of dirt removal.

With the increased archaeological interest in problems related to subsistence-settlement patterns, a demand has grown for larger, quantitatively comparable samples of smaller materials. Reconstruction of dietary patterns and environment requires seeds and bones; reconstruction of site structure requires accurate counts of debris distribution. In order to get this type of information, many field workers have begun screening the dirt removed from their excavation units. Experimental studies of the productivity of screening suggest that the decision to use screens depends on a number of factors. Among these are the scale of the operation, the time available for its completion, the locational precision desired or required, the nature and size of the material, the information sought from this material, and the rarity of the items sought. There is no clear-cut answer to the question of whether or not to screen.

Samples of various items in addition to artifacts are routinely collected during an excavation. Some of the common items samples are soil, pollen, shell, bone, and charcoal. Midden deposits can be sampled by removing a column of dirt from the side wall of a pit, or by spot-sampling, in which select squares of material are removed from top to bottom of a profile. Coring is also a useful way to obtain a sample of the general midden of a deposit. For plant and animal remains and small animal bones, water separation and flotation have been used successfully. Based on the different buoyancy of materials, these techniques use water and chemicals to hold materials in suspension so that they can be separated from the rock fraction of a midden sample. Soil samples can be collected in the same manner as midden samples and by removing hardened columns called monoliths or preparing hardened sedimentary peels. In all of these sample collection techniques, care must be exercised to safeguard the sample from contamination by adjacent materials. Nowhere is this more important than in the collection of charcoal samples for carbon dating and the recovery of pollen samples for the reconstruction of paleoenvironments.

Throughout an excavation, copious notes are taken on everything that is done and everything that is observed. The project supervisors, crew foremen, and sometimes the field workers, keep journals that record decisions and finds on a daily basis. Routine observations on individual squares, strata, levels, and samples are maintained on standardized forms. Lists of all recorded items and samples are kept to preserve a key to the provenience. All phases of work are photographed, and the individual exposures are recorded and numbered for reference purposes. Without good records, an excavation might as well not have been done, for in the notes, drawings, lists, and photos are the keys to putting the site back together again in the analytic phase.

References Cited

Ascher, Robert
  1968 Time's Arrow and the Archaeology of a Contemporary Community. In *Settlement Archaeology,* edited by K. C. Chang, pp. 43-52. Palo Alto, Calif.: National Press Books.

Barker, Graeme
  1975 To Sieve or Not to Sieve. *Antiquity* 44(193):61-63.

Biddle, Martin, and Kjolbye-Biddle, Birthe
  1969 Metres, Areas and Robbing. *World Archaeology* 1(2):208-19.

Binford, Lewis R.
  1964 A Consideration of Archaeological Research Design. *American Antiquity* 29:425-41.
  1968 Archaeological Perspectives. In *New Perspectives in Archaeology,* edited by S. R. Binford and L. R. Binford, pp. 5-32. Chicago: Aldine.

Binford, Lewis R.; Binford, S. R.; Whallon, R.; and Hardin, M. A.
  1970 Archaeology at Hatchery West. *Memoirs of the Society for American Archaeology,* No. 24.

Black, Glenn A.
  1936 Excavation of the Nowlin Mound, Dearborn County Site 7, 1934-1935. *Indiana History Bulletin* 13(7):201-342.

Black, Glenn A., and Johnston, Richard B.
  1962 A Test of Magnetometry as an Aid to Archaeology. *American Antiquity* 28:199-205.

Bordes, Francois
  1972 *A Tale of Two Caves.* New York: Harper and Row.

Braidwood, Robert J., and Howe, Bruce
  1960 *Prehistoric Investigations in Iraqui Kurdistan.* Chicago: University of Chicago Press.

Broyles, Bettye J.
  1971 Second Preliminary Report: The St. Albans Site, Kanawha County, West Virginia. *West Virginia Geological and Economic Survey, Report of Archaeological Investigations,* No. 3.

Bruder, J. Simon; Large, E. G.; and Stark, B. L.
 1975   A Test of Aerial Photography in an Estuarine Mangrove Swamp in Veracruz, Mexico. *American Antiquity* 40:330-37.
Butzer, Karl W.
 1971   *Environment and Archaeology.* Chicago: Aldine.
Byers, Douglas S. (editor)
 1967   *The Prehistory of the Tehuacan Valley.* Vol. 1: *Environment and Subsistence.* Austin: University of Texas Press.
Casteel, Richard W.
 1970   Core and Column Sampling. *American Antiquity* 35:465-67.
Chamberlin, T. C.
 1965   The Method of Multiple Working Hypotheses. *Science* 148:754-59.
Chapman, Jefferson
 1977   Archaic Period Research in the Lower Little Tennessee River Valley. *University of Tennessee Department of Anthropology Report of Investigations,* No. 18. Tennessee Valley Authority.
Chartkoff, Joseph L.
 1978   Transect Interval Sampling in Forests. *American Antiquity* 43:46-53.
Cherry, John F.
 1975   Efficient Soil Searching: Some Comments. *Antiquity* 49(195):217-19.
Chomko, Stephen A.
 1974   A Survey Technique for Delimiting Activity Areas within a Site. *Missouri Archaeological Society Newsletter,* No. 278, pp. 1-5, and No. 279, pp. 1-7.
Clark, J. G. D.
 1954   *Excavations at Star Carr.* Cambridge: At the University Press.
 1972   *Star Carr: A Case Study in Bioarchaeology.* Addison-Wesley Modular Publications, No. 10. Reading, Mass.: Addison-Wesley.
Cole, F. C., and Deuel, Thorne
 1937   *Rediscovering Illinois.* Chicago: University of Chicago Press.
Coles, John
 1972   *Field Archaeology in Britain.* London: Methuen.
Cook, S. F., and Heizer, R. F.
 1956   *Studies on the Chemical Analysis of Archaeological Sites.* University of California Publications in Anthropology, Vol. 2.
Dancey, William S.
 1974   The Archaeological Survey: A Re-orientation. *Man in the Northeast,* No. 8, pp. 98-112.
Daniel, Glyn
 1967   *The Origins and Growth of Archaeology.* Baltimore: Penguin Books.
Daniels, S. G. H.
 1972   Research Design Models. In *Models in Archaeology,* edited by David L. Clarke, pp. 201-29. London: Methuen.
Daugherty, Richard D., and Kirk, Ruth
 1976   An Ancient Indian Village Where Archaeologists Find an Avalanche Made Time Stand Still 300 Years Ago. *Smithsonian* 7(2):68-75.

Davis, Emma Lou
1975   The "Exposed Archaeology" of China Lake, California, *American Antiquity* 40:3953.

Deuel, Leo
1969   *Flights into Yesterday: The Story of Aerial Archaeology.* New York: St. Martin's Press.

Dever, William G.
1973   Two Approaches to Archaeological Method—The Architectural and the Stratigraphic. *Eretz-Israel* 11:1-8. (Jerusalem)

Dills, Charles E.
1970   Coordinate Location of Archaeological Sites. *American Antiquity* 35:389-90.

Dragoo, Don W.
1963   *Mounds for the Dead: An Analysis of the Adena Culture.* Annals of Carnegie Museum, Vol. 37.

Dubin, Robert
1969   *Theory Building.* New York: Free Press.

Dummond, D. E.
1963   A Practical Field Method for the Preservation of Soil Profiles from Archaeological Cuts. *American Antiquity* 29:116-17.

Dunnell, Robert C.
1979   Style and Function: A Fundamental Dichotomy. *American Antiquity* 43(2):192-202.

Dunnell, Robert C., and Dancey, William S.
1979   Siteless Surveys: A Regional Data Collection Strategy. Unpublished manuscript.

Dunnell, Robert C.; Campbell, S. K.; Duncan, M. A.; Lewarch, D. E.; and Rafferty, J.
1976   *Archaeological Test Excavations at the Caples Site, 45-SA-5, Skamania County, Washington.* Seattle: Department of Anthropology, University of Washington.

Edwards, Robert L.
1969   Archaeological use of the Universal Transverse Grid. *American Antiquity* 34:180-82.

Eidt, Robert C.
1973   A Rapid Chemical Field Test for Archaeological Site Surveying. *American Antiquity* 38:206-10.

Flannery, Kent V.
1968   Archaeological Systems Theory and Early Mesoamerica. In *Anthropological Archaeology in the Americas,* edited by B. Meggers, pp. 67-87. Washington, D.C.: Anthropological Society of Washington.

Flannery, Kent V. (editor)
1976   *The Early Mesoamerican Village.* New York: Academic Press.

Fowler, Melvin L.
1974   *Cahokia: Ancient Capital of the Midwest.* Addison-Wesley Modular Publications, No. 48. Reading, Mass.: Addison-Wesley.

Fry, Robert E.
1972 Manually Operated Post-hole Diggers as Sampling Instruments. *American Antiquity* 37:259-61.

Fuchs, C.; Kaufman D.; and Ronen, A.
1977 Erosion and Artifact Distribution in Open-air Epi-Paleolithic Sites on the Coastal Plain of Israel. *Journal of Field Archaeology* 4(2):171-80.

Glassow, Michael
1977 Issues in Evaluating the Significance of Archaeological Resources. *American Antiquity* 42(3)-413-20.

Greengo, Robert E.
1964 Issaquena: An Archaeological Phase in the Yazoo Basin of the Lower Mississippi Valley. *Memoirs of the Society for American Archaeology,* No. 18.

Gumerman, George J., and Lyons, Thomas R.
1971 Archaeological Methodology and Remote Sensing. *Science* 172:126-32.

Gumerman, George J., and Neely, James A.
1972 An Archaeological Survey of the Tehuacan Valley, Mexico: A Test of Color Infrared Photography. *American Antiquity* 37:520-27.

Hampton, J. N.
1975 An Experiment in Multispectral Air Photography for Archaeological Research. In *Photography in Archaeological Research,* edited by E. Harp, Jr., pp. 157-90. Albuquerque: University of New Mexico Press.

Harp, Elmer, Jr.
1974 Threshold Indicators of Culture in Air Photo Archaeology: A Case Study in the Arctic. In *Aerial Photography in Archaeological Research,* edited by E. Z. Vogt, pp. 14-27. Cambridge, Mass.: Harvard University Press.

Hayden, Julian D.
1965 Fragile Pattern Areas. *American Antiquity* 31:272-76.

Hayes, Alden, and Osborne, Douglas
1961 Fixing Site Locations by Radio-direction Finder at Mesa Verde. *American Antiquity* 27:110-12.

Hester, T. R.; Heizer, R. F.; and Graham, J. A.
1975 *Field Methods in Archaeology* (6th edition). Palo Alto, Calif.: Mayfield.

Hill, James
1968 Broken K Pueblo: Patterns of Form and Function. In *New Perspectives in Archaeology,* edited by S. R. Binford and L. R. Binford, pp. 102-43. Chicago: Aldine.

Hole, Frank, and Heizer, Robert F.
1973 *An Introduction to Prehistoric Archaeology* (3rd edition). New York: Holt, Rinehart, and Winston.

Jarman, H. N.; Legge, A. J.; and Charles, J. A.
1972 Retrieval of Plant Remains from Archaeological Sites by Froth Flotation. In *Papers in Economic Prehistory,* edited by E. S. Higgs, pp. 49-64. Cambridge: At the University Press.

Judge, W. James
1973 *PaleoIndian Occupation of the Central Rio Grande Valley in New Mexico.* Albuquerque: University of New Mexico Press.

Judge, W. James; Ebert, J. I.; and Hitchcock, R. K.
  1975   Sampling in Regional Archaeological Survey. In *Sampling in Archaeology,* edited by James W. Mueller, pp. 82-123. Tucson: University of Arizona Press.
King, Thomas E.
  1978   *The Archaeological Survey: Methods and Uses.* Heritage Conservation and Recreation Service, Cultural Resource Management Studies. Washington, D.C.: U.S. Department of the Interior.
Lastrucci, Carlo L.
  1967   *The Scientific Approach.* Cambridge, Mass.: Schenkman.
Lewis, Thomas M. N., and Kneberg, Madeline
  1946   *Hiwassee Island: An Archaeological Account of Four Tennessee Indian Peoples.* Knoxville: University of Tennessee Press.
Luchterhand, Kubet
  1970   Early Archaic Projectile Points and Hunting Patterns in the Lower Illinois Valley. *Illinois State Museum, Reports of Investigations,* No.19.
Lyons, Thomas R. (assembler)
  1976   Remote Sensing Experiments in Cultural Resource Studies. *Reports of the Chaco Center,* No. 1.
Lyons, Thomas R., and Hitchcock, Robert K. (editors)
  1977   Aerial Remote Sensing Techniques in Archaeology. *Reports of the Chaco Center,* No. 2.
McGregor, John C.
  1965   *Southwestern Archaeology.* Urbana: University of Illinois Press.
MacNeish, Richard S.
  1964   The Origins of New World Civilization. *Scientific American* 211:29-37.
Mason, Roger D.; Lewarch, Dennis E.; O'Brien, Michael J.; and Neely, James A.
  1977   An Archaeological Survey on the Xoxocotlan Piedmont, Oaxaca, Mexico. *American Antiquity* 42:567-74.
Meighan, Clement W.
  1950   Observations on the Efficiency of Shovel Archaeology. *Reports of the University of California Archaeological Survey,* No. 7, pp. 15-21.
  1969   Molluscs as Food Remains in Archaeological Sites. In *Science in Archaeology* (2nd edition), edited by D. Brothwell and E. Higgs, pp. 415-22. London: Thames and Hudson.
Millon, Rene
  1973   *Urbanization at Teotihuacan, Mexico.* Part I: *The Teotihuacan Map.* Austin: University of Texas Press.
Nelson, Charles H.
  1973   Prehistoric Culture Change in the Intermontane Plateau of Western North America. In *The Explanation of Culture Change: Models in Prehistory,* edited by Colin Renfrew, pp. 371-90. Pittsburgh: University of Pittsburgh Press.
Pendergast, David M.
  1975   The Teotihuacan Map: A Review Article. *Archaeology* 28(3):164-69.
Plog, Fred
  1974   *The Study of Prehistoric Change.* New York: Academic Press.

Plog, Stephen; Plog, Fred; and Wait, Walter
   1978   Decision Making in Modern Surveys. *Advances in Archaeological Method and Theory* 1:383-421. New York: Academic Press.

Price, John C.; Hunter R. G.; and McMichael, E. V.
   1964   Core Drilling in an Archaeological Site. *American Antiquity* 30:219:22.

Pugh, J. C.
   1975   *Surveying for Field Scientists.* Pittsburgh: University of Pittsburgh Press.

Raab, L. Mark
   1977   The Santa Rosa Wash Project: Notes on Archaeological Research Design under contract. In *Conservation Archaeology,* edited by M. P. Schiffer and G. J. Gumerman, pp. 167-82. New York: Academic Press.

Rainey, Froelich
   1971   *The Ipiutak Culture: Excavations at Point Hope, Alaska.* Addison-Wesley Modular Publications, No. 8. Reading, Mass.: Addison-Wesley.

Redman, Charles L.
   1973   Multistage Fieldwork and Analytical Techniques. *American Antiquity* 38:61-79.

Redman, Charles, L., and Watson, Patty Jo
   1970   Systematic, Intensive Surface Collection. *American Antiquity* 35:279-91.

Reed, Nelson A.; Bennett, John W.; and Porter, James W.
   1968   Solid Core Drilling of Monks Mound: Technique and Finding. *American Antiquity* 33:137-48.

Reeves, Dache M.
   1936   A Newly Discovered Extension of the Newark Works. *Ohio State Archaeological and Historical Quarterly* 45:187-93.

Roper, Donna C.
   1976   Lateral Displacement of Artifacts Due to Plowing. *American Antiquity* 41:372-75.

Sanger, David
   1970   The Archaeology of the Lochnore-Nesikep Locality, British Columbia. *Syesis,* Vol. 3, Supplement 1.

SARG
   1974   SARG: A Cooperative Approach towards Understanding the Locations of Human Settlement. *World Archaeology* 6(1):107-16.

Schiffer, Michael B.
   1972   Archaeological Context and Systematic Context. *American Antiquity* 37:156-65.
   1976   *Behavioral Archaeology.* New York: Academic Press.
   1977   Toward a Unified Science of the Cultural Past. In *Research Strategies in Historical Archaeology,* edited by Stanley South, pp. 13-40. New York: Academic Press.

Schiffer, Michael B.; Sullivan, Alan P.; and Klinger, Timothy C.
   1978   The Design of Archaeological Surveys. *World Archaeology* 10(1):1-28.

Spurling, Brian
   1976   Random and Non-random Sampling of the Same Site. In *Current Research Reports,* edited by Roy L. Carlson, pp. 57-67. Department of Anthro-

pology, Simon Fraser University, Publication No. 3, Burnaby, British Columbia.

Squier, Ephraim G., and Davis, E. H.
1848   Ancient Monuments of the Mississippi Valley. *Smithsonian Institution Contributions to Knowledge* 1.

Struever, Stuart
1968   Flotation Techniques for the Recovery of Small-Scale Archaeological Remains. *American Antiquity* 33:353-62.

Struever, Stuart, and Carlson, John
1977   Koster Site: The New Archaeology in Action. *Archaeology* 30(2):93:101.

Thomas, David H.
1974   *Predicting the Past.* New York: Holt, Rinehart and Winston.

Thomas, Peter
1975   A Response to "Pit Excavation Techniques at the Faucett Site." *Man in the Northeast,* No. 10, pp. 74-78.

Thompson, Morris M.
1979   *Maps for America.* Washington, D.C.: U.S. Department of the Interior.

Tolstoy, Paul, and Fish, Suzanne K.
1975   Surface and Subsurface Evidence for Community Size at Coapexco, Mexico. *Journal of Field Archaeology* 2:97-104.

Van der Merwe, Nikolaas J., and Stein, Pat H.
1972   Soil Chemistry of Postmolds and Rodent Burrows: Identification without Excavation. *American Antiquity* 37:245-54.

Voight, Ehrhard, and Gittens, Gayle
1977   The "Lackfilm" Method for Collecting Sedimentary Peels: Archaeological Applications. *Journal of Field Archaeology* 4(4):449-57.

Watson, Patty Jo
1976   In Pursuit of Prehistoric Subsistence: A Comparative Account of Some Contemporary Flotation Techniques. *Mid-Continental Journal of Archaeology* 1(1):77-100.

Weaver, Muriel Porter
1972   *The Aztecs, Maya, and Their Predecessors.* New York: Seminar Press.

Webb, William S., and D. L. De Jarnette
1942   *An Archaeological Survey of Pickwick Basin in Adjacent Portions of Alabama, Mississippi, and Tennessee.* Bureau of American Ethnology, Bulletin 129. Washington, D.C.: U.S. Government Printing Office.

Wheeler, Sir Mortimer
1956   *Archaeology from the Earth.* Baltimore: Penguin Books.

Willey, Gordon R., and Phillips, Philip
1958   *Method and Theory in American Archaeology.* Chicago: University of Chicago Press.

Wright, G. Ernest
1969   Archaeological Method in Palestine—An American Interpretation. *Eretz-Israel* 9:120-33. (Jerusalem)

Suggested Readings

General Archaeology

Dunnell, Robert C.
1971   *Systematics in Prehistory.* New York: Free Press.
Fagan, Brian M.
1975   *In the Beginning: An Introduction to Archaeology* (2nd edition). Boston: Little, Brown and Company.
Hole, Frank, and Heizer, Robert F.
1973   *An Introduction to Prehistoric Archaeology* (3rd edition). New York: Holt, Rinehart and Winston.
Smith, Jason W.
1976   *Foundations of Archaeology.* Beverly Hills, Calif.: Glencoe Press.

Archaeological Field Methods

Alexander, John
1970   *The Directing of Archaeological Excavations.* London: John Baker.
Crawford, O. G. S.
1954   *Archaeology in the Field.* London: Phoenix House.
Dowman, Elizabeth A.
1970   *Conservation in Field Archaeology.* London: Methuen.
Hester, T. R.; Heizer, R. F.; and Graham, J. A.
1975   *Field Methods in Archaeology* (6th edition). Palo Alto, Calif.: Mayfield.
Kenyon, Kathleen M.
1961   *Beginning in Archaeology.* New York: Praeger.
King, Thomas F.
1978   *The Archaeological Survey: Methods and Uses.* Washington, D.C.: U.S. Department of the Interior.
Webster, Graham
1974   *Practical Archaeology: An Introduction to Archaeological Field-Work and Excavation* (2nd edition). London: Adam and Charles Black.

Probability Sampling

Redman, Charles L.
   1974   *Archaeological Sampling Strategies.* Addison-Wesley Modular Publications, No. 55. Reading, Mass.: Addison-Wesley.
Mueller, James W. (editor)
   1975   *Sampling in Archaeology.* Tucson: University of Arizona Press.

Referential Systems

Greenhood, David
   1964   *Mapping.* Chicago: University of Chicago Press.
Spier, Robert F. G.
   1970   *Surveying and Mapping: A Manual of Simplified Techniques.* New York: Holt, Rinehart and Winston.

Aerial Photography

Deuel, Leo
   1969   *Flights into Yesterday: The Story of Aerial Archaeology.* New York: St. Martin's Press.
Lyons, Thomas R., and Avery, T. E.
   1977   *Remote Sensing: A Handbook for Archaeologists and Cultural Resource Managers.* Washington, D.C.: U.S. Government Printing Office.
Vogt, Evon Z. (editor)
   1974   *Aerial Photography in Anthropological Field Research.* Cambridge, Mass.: Harvard University Press.

Index

Natural units, 71-75
Newark Earthworks Site, 118-121
Nonartifactual remains, 19
Nonclustered artifact, 25, 27-28. *See also*
    Artifact
Nonsite survey, 106-112
Norms, cultural, 10
Nowlin Mound Site, 138-139
Northwest Ordinance system, 84, 93-95.
    See also UTM system

Open sites, 21
Oxidized surfaces, 133

Palynology, 163-165
Pedestalling approach, 151. *See also*
    Excavation
Phase, defined, 11, 29-30
Phosphates, and human activity, 104, 106
Photographs, 166. *See also* Aerial
    photography
Pick-matlocks, 152. *See also* Tools,
    excavation
Plane-table, 53. *See also* Compass; Transit
Planimetric (two-dimensional) recording
    systems, 75
Pollen sampling, 163-165
Pompeii mentality, 28-29
Post-hole testing, 130-131
Potassium-argon dating, 2
Potsherd, 76. *See also* Artifact
Precision, in archaeology, 63
Primary observation form, 165-166
Primary sites, 22
Probability sampling, 46-48
Probing, 128-129
Problem formulation, 39-44
Processual archaeology, 2-3, 6
Projectile points, 27-29. *See also* Artifact
Proposition, 7, 8-9
Proton magnometry, 106
Provenience, defined, 75
Pueblo ruins, 73-74

Quadrant method, 147, 149-150. *See also*
    Excavation
Quadrat, 84. *See also* Grid
Quartering method, 147. *See also*
    Excavation

Radar, 124
Radio frequency receiver, 124
Radiocarbon dating, 2, 163-164
Radio-direction finder, 94
Rainey, Froelich, 116

Recording tool kit, 154
Records, excavation, 165-169
Recovery operations, 54-60
    actual versus expected, 60
    of artifacts, 57
Redman, Charles L., and Patty Jo Watson,
    101
Redman model for recovery, 57-59
Reese River Valley Site, 67-68, 70
Referential systems, 51
Region, defined, 13
Remote sensing, 123-124, 126

St. Albans Site, 131-133
Samples, collecting, 157-159
Samples, soil, 104-105
Sampling design, 45-51
Sampling units, 37
SARG (Southwest Anthropological
    Research Group), 45
Scheffer, Michael, 32
Scientific method, 6-8
Scintillation counters, 123-124
Screening, 154-157
Secondary sites, 22
Sectioning approach, 151. *See also*
    Excavation
Sedimentary peel, 161-163
Shadow mark, 114. *See also* Signatures
Shoshone lifeways, 67-68
Shovel testing, 129
Shoveling and screening, compared, 154-157
Signatures, 114, 116-117
Site, 13, 20, 21. *See also specific site names*
    closed, 21
    defined, 13
    designation, 88, 93
    location, 93-96
    names, 93
    open, 21
    subsurface, 21-22
    surface, 21-22
Site survey, 88-98
    forms, 88-92
    intensive examination in, 98-106
    method of discovery, 97-98
Smithsonian Institution River Basin Survey
    system, 93
Soil mark, 114. *See also* Signatures
Soil monolith, 161
Soil sampling, 160-161
Soil testing and mapping, 104
Soil-mixing processes, 34
Spatial organization, 13-15. *See also* Site
Star Carr Site, 42-43